THE MANTRA OF PEACEFUL POLITICS

SEVEN
PRESCRIPTIONS
BY DR. CALM

iBooks

Habent Sua Fata Libelli

iBooks
Manhanset House
Shelter Island Hts., New York 11965-0342

bricktower@aol.com • www.ibooksinc.com
All rights reserved under the International and Pan-American Copyright
Conventions. No part of this publication may be reproduced, stored in a retrieval
system, or transmitted in any form or by any means, electronic, or otherwise, without
the prior written permission of the copyright holder.
The iBooks colophon is a registered trademark of
J. Boylston & Company, Publishers.

Library of Congress Cataloging-in-Publication Data
Dintyala, Kiran
The Mantra of Peaceful Politics—Seven Prescriptions By Dr. Calm
p. cm.

1. Political Science—Political Process—Campaigns & Elections.
2. Political Science—Comparative Politics.
3. Political Science—Political Process—Political Parties. 4. United States—
Non-Fiction
Non-Fiction, I. Title.
ISBN: 978-1-899694-23-5 Trade Paper

August 2024

THE MANTRA OF PEACEFUL POLITICS

SEVEN
PRESCRIPTIONS BY DR. CALM

Kiran Dintyala MD, MPH

Acknowledgments

I am thankful to all the people involved in publishing of this book in such a short period.

First and foremost, I acknowledge the fact that I wouldn't have been able to write a single word of inspiration without the intuitive guidance provided by God and the teachings of my guru Sri Paramahansa Yogananda. Their constant presence is the guiding force of my life and an eternal source of inspiration, strength, and courage to pursue all my endeavors.

I am deeply indebted to Mr. Alan Morell, my agent and manager, for his support in getting this book published.

I thank Mr. John Colby, founder and the president of Brick Tower Press, for giving me an opportunity to be published by their prestigious publishing house and be ready to work on a very tight deadline to bring this book to life.

I am deeply indebted to my parents and my sister for their steadfast love and support.

Last but not the least, my daughter, Mayura, who gives meaning to my life and inspires me every day to progress and prosper in life and in her beautiful ways, reminds me to live life to the fullest every moment. Without her, I am not there. Her love for me and my love for her is what keeps me going in life.

Disclaimer

The goal of this book is to help people find calm during this election season. As an advocate of peace, I am neutral to either parties, Democrats or Republicans. I am neither pro-Trump nor against Trump. I believe in moderation in all aspects of life and so in politics too. Extremism in any form is dangerous and leads to misery in the end.

In certain parts of the book, it may appear that I am supporting or refuting either parties' policies or philosophies. It's done for the sake of discussion and to help the reader comprehend the current political divide. But if you consider the book as a whole, it maintains a neutral tone.

Whether you are a Never-Trumper or Forever Trumper, I respect you and I believe you have the right to support anyone you wish to. Regardless of your political affiliation, if you sincerely apply the teachings in this book, you will find calm during this election season and beyond.

Thank You.

Table of Contents

Preface

I still remember the upheaval that our nation went through during the last two election cycles, in 2016 and 2020. It seems the trend continues in 2024... everywhere chaos regarding the election, especially after the first debate between the two presidential candidates on June 27th, 2024.

President Biden's performance in the debate threw the entire Democrat party into a panic mode.

On the other side, Republicans are anxious and worried, despite Mr. Donald Trump's performance because of his recent conviction.

We are seeing a tremendous amount of stress and conflict in our already divided nation.

Families are fighting at the dinner table...friendships are falling apart.

There is HIGH TENSION everywhere with anxiety, higher blood pressure, and palpitations.

But this is not just during Trump era; elections have been a source of great stress from time immemorial and will continue to be.

So, the principles laid out in this book are not ephemeral either. They are timeless and are applicable no matter where the elections are local, national, or international.

The stakes are high! The emotions are up for a roller-coaster ride!

What do you do?

How can you stay **Calm in The Midst of Chaos,** during this election cycle?

How can you save your relationships and protect your health from election stress?

How to stay peaceful despite the never-ending negative news cycle?

How can you be happy and prosperous no matter who your President is?

Who do you vote for?

If you are serious about finding answers to your questions... read this book!

FIND CALM and VOTE RIGHT!

Introduction

Note: Though the book is written in the backdrop of 2024 elections, the principles behind the material discussed in this book is applicable to any election in general.

The American Psychological Association (APA) survey of 2000 adults, conducted in April 2024 showed 73% of Americans are worried about the upcoming election. https://www.psychiatry.org/News-room/News-Releases/Annual-Poll-Adults-Express-Increasing-Anxiousness

As the 2024 Presidential elections inch closer, chaos, confusion, and fear are unfolding on both Republican and Democratic fronts. From politicians to the voters, everyone is feeling anxious as their fates unravel over the next few months.

The polls, the talk shows, the constant chatter on radio, the explosive news articles on the likes of New York Times and other major magazines, the social media frenzy, and the overall toxic political climate greatly accelerates the tensions and anxieties of an already divided nation, gripped with fear because of inflation, recession, war and more. Not only that, the prospect of losing social security benefits, the failing health care system, the ballooning up national debt, the opioid epidemic, and many other unsolved, deeply troubling problems are anxiety provoking and directly impact the voters at an individual level deep through their hearts and minds – threatening their physical, mental, financial, and social well-being.

The first presidential debate between President Biden and former President Trump on June 27th 2024 did nothing to alleviate these concerns, for most part. On the contrary, it was quite anxiety provoking for the millions who watched it.

During these extremely difficult times, people need a way to find solace and peace despite the increasing tumult. They need reassurance that all will be alright no matter what the political outcome might look like at this time. They need guidance – someone to hold their hand and show them a way out of this chaos. They need to focus back on their lives, jobs, and other important things in life, so that they could prosper and progress. They need help to let go of the negative emotions about this obnoxious political climate and find harmony with their family and friends despite the ideological differences.

All in all, they need to find **Calm in the Midst of Chaos** so that they can stay sane during the day, sleep at night, and find a balanced way to handle the political turmoil they face each day.

Key takeaways from this book:

1. **Realizing that true happiness lies within.** Moving away from conditional happiness to unconditional happiness, so that no matter what the circumstances are you can be happy.

2. **Your prosperity depends 90% on your efforts and 10% on your circumstances.** So, if you put in the right effort in the right way, you will prosper no matter what your circumstances are. So, your future is in your hands.

3. **Overcoming negativity and quickly calming down your emotions** is going to be an essential skill to be mastered by all who want to wither this election cycle. With powerful tools and techniques in this book, you could do that in a matter of minutes, wherever and whenever you want.

4. **Learn to be forgiving towards yourself as well as others.** It's going to heal your heart faster than you think. Without forgiveness, we can't survive as humanity because human beings are full of misunderstandings, miscommunications, and mistakes.

5. **Do the right thing. But more importantly do so in a kind way.** Righteousness without kindness is like doing

surgery without anesthesia. The subject will be flailing and fighting even though you are trying to help. *Always apply the Calm Balm to the Sharp Edges of Your Righteous Knife.*

6. Empty your mind before going to bed. Do not let the troubles and worries of the day encroach into the night. Let your mind rest in peace for a refreshing and rejuvenating sleep.

7. Develop even-mindedness. There will always be positive and negative things in life. Don't let your emotions swing widely with the circumstances. The more you practice this, the more poised you will be.

Read on...

Chapter 1
TrumperTension vs. BidenMentia

It's June 2024, the day after Trump vs. Biden debate on CNN.

"Doctor, doctor!" the nurse was talking to the doctor over the phone, "this patient's blood pressure is dangerously high. It's 220/110. I already gave him his morning medications but still, I can't control it. He is anxious, having palpitations, and reporting crushing chest pain that's 10/10 intensity."

Dr. Calm had to run immediately to the ward where the patient was. He quickly examined the patient. Started him on a blood pressure medication through the intravenous route, some aspirin by mouth, and a nitroglycerin tablet to put under his tongue. In a few minutes, the patient's blood pressure improved, and his chest pain subsided, but his anxiety is not alleviated yet.

The doctor sat next to him, holding his hand, and asked "What happened?" "Have you been taking all the blood pressure medications regularly?"

The patient answered, "Yes, I am."

"Have you been consuming extra salt to your diet?" the doctor inquired.

"No, I am not" replied the patient.

"Then, what's causing your blood pressure to be so high? Few months ago, your blood pressure was well controlled with these same meds" the doctor was thinking aloud.

The patient was looking perplexed.

The doctor continued, "Have you been stressed about anything? You look quite anxious."

The patient keeps quiet.

The doctor continues, "Something must be going on. There must be a reason for your blood pressure to shoot up like that. It's nothing to do with medications or diet. If you tell me what's going on, I could help."

Finally, the anxious looking patient opens his mouth, "I don't know. But I have been feeling anxious for the past few months. There is so much turmoil all around. There is so much negativity. These politics are terrible. I feel like this nation is being destroyed by these political fights between Democrats and Republicans. Every time I turn on the television, my mind goes crazy, my heart races fast, and my thoughts run wild. All that news is anxiety provoking. It never stops. The negative news cycle is constantly on. I don't know how to pull myself out of it. I don't know how to stay at peace with myself and with all that's going on."

The doctor looked into the patient's eyes. There is deep pain in there. He looked very worried and seemed genuinely concerned about himself, the society, and the future of the nation.

Dr. Calm places his hand reassuringly on the patient's shoulder and said smilingly, "Everything will be alright. I know what's causing this. It's either TrumperTension or BidenMentia!"

The patient looked at the doctor quizzically.

Dr. Calm continued, "It's your severe anxiety that's causing you the palpitations, the blood pressure to shoot up so high, and have the chest pain too. Quite a number of people have been experiencing these symptoms since the 2016 Presidential election. People have been reporting a variety of symptoms like yours, including chest pains, high blood pressure, palpitations, heart attacks, severe panic attacks, and much more since Mr. Trump became our president followed by Mr. Biden in 2020. Sometimes people are feeling like they are losing their minds, as if they got dementia. The two candidates running for the president are evoking these symptoms in millions of people."

"Don't get me wrong. I am not saying that Mr. Trump or Mr. Biden is causing all these symptoms. I am simply saying that this phenomenon has started since Mr. Trump became our president, followed by Mr. Biden. They may or may not have been responsible for your symptoms - that depends on your political affiliation.

If you are a Republican, you are enraged about why the Democrats can't let Mr. Trump be at peace. They tried to endanger his Presidency from day one with White House leaks, the Russian investigation, and false propaganda about him and his family. They pushed him into a legal quagmire with multiple cases against him, to derail his candidacy for running President again. You are afraid that Biden may have dementia and lacks the capability to run the nation smoothly and safely.

If you are a Democrat, you are furious about Trump's personality and inflammatory messages. You are afraid of the Republican policies that endanger our environment, accelerating the Global Warming. You just can't understand how our nation elected Mr. Trump as our President and he is a big threat to our democracy if he runs again.

But, regardless of political affiliation, both sides of the aisle have been feeling these symptoms for different reasons. It's 24-hour TRUMP and hostile politics on TV and the way the news is being reported is anxiety provoking. It's literally driving people insane. This amount of negativity on news channels was never seen before. The amount of hostility is unparalleled. Every time people turn on TV, they are having the conglomeration of all these symptoms. For the lack of a better word to describe it medically, I coined the term TrumperTension."

The patient was looking at the doctor unbelievably. A faint smile appeared on his face, even in the midst of all this anxiety. It's the word **TrumperTension** that made him smile. He couldn't suppress his smile. Then he started laughing almost uncontrollably. "I didn't know that there are so many out there with the same symptoms...I mean TrumperTension. Hats off to your sense of humor doc! You found a way to take a very serious problem and put it into a term that makes us laugh!"

The patient's feeling lighter. His blood pressure is almost back to normal and his anxiety is slowly dissolving.

The patient continued, "I know I am feeling lighter and better. That's good. But once I go back home, I am sure the TrumperTension is going to be back. I don't know how to handle all that stress. I don't know how to stay calm in the midst of all this chaos."

Dr. Calm continued, "You will be alright. I am totally confident about it. I know you are worried, but I assure you that we will work together on this. Come see me in my office, next week. We will talk more."

With that, the patient feeling reassured, goes home.

A week later the patient comes back to see the doctor.

Dr. Calm inquires, "How have you been doing?"

"Feeling much better doc. My blood pressure is under control. No more palpitations. But I still feel anxious about all the crazy things going around. Only if there is a way to keep my anxiety under control, I will feel happier. Can you prescribe me some anxiety pills?" asked the patient.

The doctor replies, "Okay, I could prescribe you pills but that's only going to help you temporarily. Moreover, these psychiatric medications have many side effects. Would you be willing to try a different approach where you don't become dependent on pills?"

"What's that approach?" asked the patient eagerly.

"It's called Dr. Calm's Method for Stress-Free Living."

"What's that doc?"

"It's about understanding stress and uncovering where it comes from in our life. It's about attacking the root cause of stress rather than superficially dealing with it. It's about equipping you with the tools to dissolve stress and find peace, joy, and balance in your life.

It's simply not about someone counseling you or telling you what to do but empowering you with powerful ways to remain calm no matter what your situation is.

It's not merely managing stress. It's about eliminating it. It's about preventing it. All your anxieties, fears, worries, and insecurities in life can come to an end.

Once you learn this new method, you will be equipped with the necessary knowledge, tools, and resources that will stay with you for life."

"Wow! That sounds exciting to me doc. I would like to try this new approach, but I have a question. How quickly will I get the results?'

"Well, if you sincerely apply these teachings, you will see good results quickly. I have people with years of anxiety, worry, and other mental health issues that got resolved in a matter of few days. I don't want to overpromise, but I have some clients who saw massive positive results within the first hour of our interaction."

"Your words are very encouraging doc, but I am still skeptical. Maybe it's going to work for small problems, but I am not sure if it's going to work for major problems like TrumperTension, with so much chaos and turmoil around. I already tried psychotherapy, counseling, and even some anxiety pills in the past without much avail. Please tell me how this helps. Give me a couple of examples of stress getting resolved and situations that got better with this approach of yours."

With that, Dr. Calm paused for a moment and then said with a reassuring smile, "The Principles and Techniques you are going to learn are Universal. They work with mathematical accuracy. The more you understand and practice them, the better your results will be. You are doubting them because you haven't experienced them.

Let me share with you a real-life story of how these principles and techniques worked magic."

The patient's eagerly listening...

Chapter 2
Finding Calm in the Midst of Chaos

The beginning of calm in my life – True Story

"I was having a panic attack. At least it appeared to be so with my hands shaking, mind anxious, and heart racing. My whole-body's sweating as if I was running a marathon in hot summer. But, in fact, it's chilly out there, everything covered with snow, and I was sitting on the floor in my tiny dorm room, with a laptop resting on a cheap wooden desk in front of me. I was aghast, looking at the single most important piece of information that I have been waiting eagerly for two years. I had prepared well. I had been confident. I had given all I could. And yet, this terrible news stuck me like a lightning. It means, my lifelong dreams of becoming a doctor will be coming to an end. It means, my hard work for the past many years will go in vain. It means, I have lost not only two precious years in my career but have also accrued a $25,000 debt which was insurmountable for me at that point of time. I will have to go back to India and start all over again! What a shame! What will my friends say? How can I show my face to my family? I have let down everyone who believed in me! A zillion thoughts were restlessly dancing in my mind enveloping me in a cloud of negativity, making me feel totally distraught and destroyed. That day was March 13th, 2007. The day that changed everything!

I came from an average, middle class family in India. To give you a little background of how dire my financial situation was when I embarked on this journey to come to the United States in 2005, my father didn't have even a thousand dollars to buy me a flight ticket. He had to borrow from his friends. At that time, he told me, "I was barely able to get a loan from the bank to pay for your first semester fee. After that, you have to sustain yourself there or else you will have to come back. And remember we will be in huge debt if you come back emptyhanded. And I wouldn't know how to pay it off." I nodded my head, unaware of the perils awaiting me in this journey. My father must have had a lot of trust in me to spend his last penny and also borrow a sizeable loan so that I could build a bright career.

Young and energetic, beaming with confidence, the moment I landed in the United States, I was on a mission to succeed! To make my dreams come true! To become a doctor here! I don't know how but from a very young age, I was always confident about my ability to succeed no matter what, though sometimes oblivious to the risks and challenges involved in the process.

So, I worked hard, I made things happen that were not possible for my fellow students, at a much faster pace than expected. I think it's my strong will to succeed that propelled me like a jet, swiftly towards my goals, crossing the mountains of challenges. Yet, after two years of hard work and persistence, for the first time in my life, I was at the doorstep of major failure. I was denied access to become a doctor here in the United States, despite excellent credentials. I couldn't understand why. What's gone wrong? What is it? It's unusual. It should be a breeze for someone with my credentials. At least it was so until last year. This year, there is something strange going on.

No matter the reason, the harsh realities of life have finally caught up with me. Until this moment, I was this buoyant young man, bubbling with confidence, always happy and optimistic. And all of a sudden, I was feeling totally deflated, defeated by the circumstance, with the prospect of failure weighing on me heavily. It felt as if someone has hurled me out of a fast-moving Ferrari and I fell flat on my face with full force. Totally broken mentally and emotionally! I was feeling dazed and confused. Over the next few days as the news continued to sink in, I was feeling more and more terrible. Prior to that, I never knew that one could feel so low.

Negative thoughts enveloped me like a storm. I didn't feel like talking to anyone. I was afraid to share the news with family and friends. Only my roommate knew. I was sitting there feeling lonely and isolated. Eventually my family and friends came to know about the situation. Everyone consoled me and yet no one could give me the answers to understand why this happened. Everyone supported me but still couldn't take away the pain and anguish I was going through. I was thinking, "If hard work, persistence, and intelligent workings can't help a man to accomplish his goals, then what could? What's missing in me? What is it that I have to learn?" That was the burning question I had in my mind at that time and no one could answer it.

I sought the counsel of friends, family, colleagues, and many others, desperate for answers. They didn't have answers either. Actually, some of those discussions made me feel even more confused. I started going to the university library, looking for answers but didn't know which books to read. I randomly picked a few books. They helped a little bit but still didn't answer my questions. I was an avid reader while I was in med school and read 'The Magic of Thinking Big, The Seven Habits of Highly Effective People, Unlimited Power, Awaken the Giant Within, Fountain Head, Dale Carnegie, and many other great books written by influential authors.' They were helpful to me until this time but even with all that knowledge, still I was falling short of answers.

I didn't know where to go. So, I started reading scriptures for a little while. That's beyond my threshold because I was never into spirituality or religion. Having a scientific bent of mind from a young age, I have not seen the spiritual side of life as something worth considering. Even though I started reading scriptures, I could barely understand the meaning imbibed in them. As weeks passed by, my situation became more and more hopeless. My quest for finding answers came to a standstill.

If this continues, I will have to go back to India in three months as my visa will expire and I wouldn't have money to continue beyond that. Either I will have to find a way to secure my position as a doctor in one of the residency programs or get ready to be deported. It's a do or die situation.

Every passing minute made my anxieties only worse. There was time pressure, tremendous time pressure.

I am a very optimistic person to begin with, but I started losing it. I was hanging by one tiny thread of hope. There must be an answer. There must be an answer. So, I started looking for answers on the internet but it's of no avail either. (At that time, internet was not really the primary way for people to find answers. Google was not that widespread). I was ready to give up. Six weeks passed and I have tried all that I could and came to a dead end.

I was sitting there in my dorm, and it was around 2:30 pm on a Friday afternoon. I was counting how much money is there in my bank account for my expenses for the next three months. I was wondering if I will have enough money left to buy a flight ticket back to India. My visa will expire soon. With that thought, again I started panicking. My thoughts were chaotic.

As I was sitting there, even in the midst of all that chaos, I didn't know how, but somewhere from deep within I suddenly remembered that there's a professor in the University that teaches stress management. I didn't know much about her at that time, but I knew that if I don't go get some help soon, I will be going totally crazy.

So, I quickly I got up, walked down the dorm steps, and hastily walked to the University, 20 minutes away. I started looking around and found the professor's office. The door was closed. I knocked at it hesitantly and the assistant answered the door, "Do you have an appointment?" I hurriedly exclaimed, "No! But I need to talk with her urgently." She replied, "Okay, please sit down. I will get the professor."

As, I sat down nervously, professor Judith Sedgeman greeted me welcomingly. She inquired how she could be of help. Without wasting time, I quickly blurted out what's going on and shared with her the miserable situation I had been in. She listened carefully, and said with a reassuring tone, "Everything will be alright. Stay calm." I was thinking in my mind, "But how? How to stay calm? I don't know how!"

She spoke with me for a few minutes, but my mind was so restless that I barely registered what she was saying. And then I heard her saying, "I have a class to teach in a couple of minutes. I have to go."

I was disappointed to hear that. I was thinking in the back of my mind, "Ugh! Can't she wait for a few more minutes and help me? What's the big deal if she is late to the class? My situation is really urgent!" But I helplessly watched her go back into her room and a minute later she returned with some reading material and a CD to listen to. She kindly said, "Everything will be alright. We will talk again later. Please stay in touch."

I remember that moment. I was feeling totally lost, not knowing what to do next. Sadly, with a heavy heart I walked out of the office building. I stood there for a few minutes. I was feeling hungry as I missed my lunch. Didn't eat breakfast either as I didn't feel like having one. I slowly started walking back to my dorm with tear filled eyes. I stopped by at McDonald's on the way, got a small sandwich that I could barely eat. It just didn't taste right. Slowly, I dragged myself to the dorm. Threw my backpack onto the floor. I didn't know what to do. I looked at the material my professor gave me.

Honestly, I didn't have anything better to do. So, casually I started perusing through the material. I tried to read but my thoughts were so restless, flying in a thousand directions that I could barely concentrate. And this is someone who aced in USMLE (Medical Licensing Exam to become a doctor).

So, I had to put away the reading material. There was a CD next to it. Fortunately, my roommate had a CD player. I borrowed it and put on the headphones. I really had no expectations. And as I started listening to the audio, somewhere around 15 minutes or so, I started feeling something different...at that time I didn't know how to describe it...I was feeling some kind of lightness in my heart. I was feeling peaceful. I was feeling almost like a void within. It's as if someone has taken a vacuum cleaner and sucked out all the negative thoughts out of mind. Just prior to that, my thoughts were running at a million miles per second. But suddenly, all those racing thoughts have come to an abrupt halt as if someone applied strong brakes on them. My mind has come to a STAND STILL.

At that time, I was thinking in my mind, "I don't know what this is, but it feels good. For some reason, I am not feeling worried anymore." It was a strange but good experience. It's strange because none of my circumstances changed. Just a few minutes prior I was feeling terribly stressed and my life was falling apart. And yet, just a few minutes later, I was feeling at peace as if nothing had happened in the past few months. As if everything is alright. I liked that feeling. So, I continued to listen...probably for another 5 minutes. And something even more inexplicable happened. I started feeling joyful. Yes, I was feeling joyful. I couldn't understand it. How could someone feel happy when everything around them is wrong. It's just not possible. With that thought, fear came to me. "Am I really going crazy?" Thinking that, I immediately put down the CD player.

I ran to the phone and quickly dialed my professor's number. Fortunately, she picked up the phone. Seems she had just finished the class. I quickly explained her what's happened and asked, "Am I going crazy?" She laughed and said, "Of course, no! You are doing alright."

She explained, "That's what happens when you access your innate health. It's your natural state of mental wellbeing where your happiness is not dependent on external circumstances. Your peace of mind is with you always. It's just a matter of accessing it. And these Principles you heard just helped you access that deep peace and joy you already have within."

I felt relieved to hear that there's nothing wrong with me. But that experience changed everything for me. For the next few days, my newfound peace and joy was unshakeable. I walked as if I have no problems. Mingled around with friends like before. I was not worried what they're thinking about me. I had no fear of the future. I was just a happy being.

Almost, at the same time, Melissa, a relatively new friend of mine, having learnt about my situation offered me a small booklet on meditation. Prior to that I never meditated. Well, I tried once a few years ago but miserably failed. So, I was skeptical. Again, as I was desperate, I was ready to try literally anything. It was around 7:30 pm in the evening. I walked back to the dorm room. I read the meditation technique. It's foreign to me. I tried to understand it the best I could, closed the door shut for some quiet, and sat down to meditate. 10-15 min passed by. I was not sure whether I was doing it right or not, but something started feeling different in me. It's hard to explain. It felt like all the restless thoughts in my mind are subsiding. It felt like some clarity dawning in my mind. I felt a deep CALM. At that time, I didn't have the right words to describe it but all I felt was something good. There's a feeling of inner security. This was almost the same feeling I felt when I was listening to the Principles on the audio.

What happened next was something that no one expected. Over the next 3 months a series of miracles happened, taking me from one place to the other, one opportunity to another, and finally I was able to secure a position as a resident doctor in a prestigious training program. My visa issues resolved. My financial problems dissolved. All the anxieties and worries vanished. I was ecstatic. Everyone was happy for me – my friends, family, colleagues, and everyone around me. They just couldn't believe I made it. Under normal circumstances this achievement would not be possible for least another 1-2 years and that too with a lot of time, energy, and money to be spent.

So, I came out victorious in a do or die situation. The impossible became possible. Many good things followed after this victory. (To do justification to what happened in those 3 months and explain it properly without losing the suspense and excitement, it would require an entire new book, which I will write in the future).

During that time, I realized that it is the **deep calmness** within that guided me to the right places at the right time to the right opportunities and unfolded the exciting future I am destined to reach. I realized that:

- If you can find **'calm in the midst of chaos'** no problem
is unsurmountable.

- **Calmness combined with strong will** and hard work can **shatter the prison walls of limitations** around you.
- **Calmness is the greatest catalyst** for true success and happiness in life.
- And, to **find peace of mind all it takes is just one moment.** That moment can happen any time.
- It is **a misnomer that it takes years to find peace.** If you are ready, you can find peace now!

With that newfound power of calmness, I set myself off on to a new path – to delve deep into the science and art of calmness and further explore the possibilities. I dedicated many long hours for a number of years to learn, experiment, and research to make sure that what I experienced is not a one-time thing, not a sporadic experience but the results are reproducible at will. To answer my question, the universe has given me enough troubles over the next few years. Many of these happened in a quick succession at regular intervals as if the Universe was trying to toughen me up, accelerate the process of my growth, and deepen my ability to remain CALM IN THE MIDST OF CHAOS. It is as if I was being prepared to serve a greater mission: that is to help my fellow human beings to FIND CALM in their lives; to help them FIGHT STRESS and WIN THE BATTLE OF LIFE. Over a decade, I have refined these teachings to the highest level and made them as simple as possible for people to follow them and get fast results, instead of reinventing the wheel by themselves.

As I started sharing my new learnings, I found that it doesn't matter who I am interacting with and what the situation was – people always found CALM whether I talked to them one-on-one or in a group setting; whether I was conducting a seminar, or they were reading a book or listening to an audio. These PRINCIPLES and TECHNIQUES work with mathematical accuracy whether it is my life or my clients' lives! It's really fascinating to see this phenomenon happen again and again. Even more importantly, it's very rewarding to my soul to see the positive results in others' lives – the primary reason why I chose to become a doctor," finished Dr. Calm.

The patient who was sitting there listening to the story all this time quietly, clears his throat to say, "Doc, thanks for sharing your miraculous story. It's an eye-opener for me. I am in. Tell me what I need to do next. I will follow these Principles and Techniques."

Chapter 3
The Millennial's Dilemma

**A conversation between a millennial grandson and
his grandfather advising him.**

It's June 2024. With the advent of summer and the prospect of having some time off, Johnny should be feeling elated and excited. Instead, he was feeling down. Feeling beat up. Every year Johnny would do something special during the summer holidays whether revisiting his hobbies, taking a road trip, or something else that's fun and exciting... but this time... he literally couldn't get himself up to do anything. There is too much going on in his mind. This is not his usual self. He is normally a cheerful young man who likes to enjoy time with friends, go out with family, and volunteer to serve the poor and challenged. Yet, none of those activities have interested him the past few weeks.

The past few weeks, he has been following all that's been happening about the possible conviction of Trump, the economic recession, the bombings in Gaza with innocent children dying...Seems he just can't escape bad news. Whether it his parents, his roommate, or someone else watching TV, he would get pulled into the negative news cycle inadvertently. If he managed to escape the TV, he would still get exposed to the political turmoil on social media. If not that, at college someone would comment on Trump, leading to an hourlong unpleasant discussion about who is right and who is wrong.

"I need to find a way back to my normal self. I can't continue to worry like this. I got to solve this problem or else I am going to go crazy," pacing back and forth in his room, Johnny was seriously thinking what he should do this summer. After much thought, he comes to a decision. "You know what, I am going to go visit grandpa! He has always been fun to spend time with and he is wise. He always helped me find solutions to my problems...big or small. Moreover, he has been asking me to visit his place for a while." With that thought, he quickly packs the luggage for a weeklong trip to grandpa.

Grandpa is happy to see Johnny but immediately notices that he is not his normal self. He inquires, "Johnny what happened? Anything wrong?"

"I will tell you everything this evening Grandpa. I am a little tired now."

As they sit together to eat supper that evening, Johnny opens up. "Last four years have been really rough grandpa. Seeing all that has been happening since the 2020 election cycle, I am worried about the future of the nation, my future, the college debt, rising healthcare costs, global wars, social unrest, the inequalities and racism, national debt, running out of resources, social security funds, and more...How am I going to survive all this chaos? My future looks dire. I feel like crying. My friends feel the same too. None of us millennials feel that we have a chance to do well in our lives. We constantly message each other and talk on social media about how terrible the outlook is for our generation.

One of my fellow students, Billy attempted a suicide recently. He was taken to the hospital and resuscitated. His parents were totally devastated. They blame themselves for his fate because they don't know how to guide him. They feel helpless themselves.

My friend's mother Nelly is an educated woman but a **Confused Republican** under constant consternation about her allegiance to the Republican party and Mr. Trump's actions. She feels guilty voting for him and yet feels that the Republican party is the only one that can help this nation. She can't imagine losing to Democrats and Biden winning again. She doesn't believe that Democrat policies are going to help the nation. Billy's father Willy is a **Resentful Democrat.** He has been a lifelong Democrat and he used to get along reasonably well with his Republican wife until recently. And once he found that she voted for TRUMP, his relationship with her was never the same.

They tried to put aside their political differences, but every time he imagines how Trump could destroy the nation (in his opinion), his blood boils and ears fume. He becomes very resentful and gets into a fight with his wife. He constantly watches Rachel Maddow on MSNBC and Anderson Cooper on CNN and fumes at TRUMP. Nelly loves The FIVE and Sean Hannity on FOXNEWS and the way they rip apart Democrats! After they watch the shows, every night they start discussion at the dinner table, trying to convince each other why their perspective is right. Every night they try to find dominion over each other and end up almost fist fighting.

My poor friend Billy is totally frustrated by the constant conflict he must witness at home. Seems, he has been growing up like this all his childhood, but it really got worse past 4 years. He feels his parents have no time for him. As a millennial, he has his own opinions, but his parents are totally deaf to them. He doesn't feel understood at home. He doesn't feel cared for. All he feels is frustration. He didn't know what to do with himself. He fell to bad company and started using drugs, which have taken a toll on him. When his parents found out about this, he didn't know what to do... so he thought suicide is the best way to end his problems.

I know many of my friends are frustrated about the whole situation with our President and where the country is going and how their future looks. I don't know what to do grandpa! I feel terrible too! At home, my mom and dad are a little reserved when it comes to discussion of politics before me, but I know they have their differences too. But they are too busy trying to get their bills paid. They don't have enough time to fight, like Billy's rich parents. Maybe it's a good thing that we are not rich. My head is spinning just thinking about all this stuff and I don't know what to do or who to share with all this stuff. Thank God, I could visit you and spend some time here. I always liked you since I was a little kid. You always had answers for my questions. I am hoping you could help me with this too!

Grandpa, sitting poised in his chair, has been listening intently for almost an hour trying to understand Johnny's problems. He quickly recognized that behind his grandson's frustrated ramble, there is some intelligent thought process. In fact, because he is a smart and intelligent kid trying to make sense of this chaotic world, he is so confused. To someone who is not thinking about the issues this much, they will be less concerned. That's the reason, *ignorance is bliss!*

His questions are spot-on to some of the deepest problems this nation is facing at the moment. These are not just his concerns but of millions of people who are worried about the divided nation and their future. Drugs, gun shootings, border crisis, trade war, and political frenzy are made more volatile by media sensationalism. The negative news spreading like wildfire on social media is consuming not only the mental health of millions around the world but also is resulting in physical illnesses because of the sheer amount of stress people are facing each day.

The common man is totally feeling out of control and out of his elements in these uncertain times. There is insecurity, fear, and despair not only in our nation but all around the world. The world cannot be viewed anymore as independent nations divided by their boundaries. The information revolution and advanced communication have changed this world into a small HITECH VILLAGE where the news from even the most remote locations can spread rapidly across the continents in minutes.

Grandpa feels sad for his grandson and the generation of millennials facing angst during these tumultuous times. He remembers being a victim of the 2016 election stress and at that time he saw Dr. Calm for counsel and that changed his life forever. Since then, he has been applying his teachings religiously and that has kept him out of trouble. He decides to take those teachings and help his grandchild, his parents, as well as his friend.

Grandpa is lost in thought, "Whatever solution I come up with should help not only my grandson but all the nation. If I just counsel him, he will, benefit from it but it will stop there. But I want this message to be spread to millions of people looking for answers. How do I do that?" There's a period of silence as he was thinking all this. Both Johnny and grandpa are lost in thought in their own minds in their own worlds.

And then came an idea...in fact a brilliant idea and he quickly starts putting it to action. He gets up from his chair and walks into the next room. Johnny startled by this sudden movement...wonders what's going on in grandpa's mind. He follows him... Grandpa is getting ready to go out.

"Grandpa, what's going on? asks Johnny."

"Give me a minute. Will explain you shortly," says grandpa excitingly. "First things first! Let's go see your friend Billy at the hospital."

Chapter 4
The Suicide Mission –
Finding Hope in the Pit
of Misery

"It's our thinking about the situation rather than the situation itself that's responsible for how we feel about it."

Grandpa takes his grandson and visits Billy and his family at the hospital. Billy lying down in the bed makes a faint attempt to smile. His eyes look tired and sad, his words projecting total hopelessness. Grandpa realizes that it's not going to be easy to lift him out of despair. He is living in a pit of misery. Already the psychiatrists and therapists tried to help him without much success. It's going to be a suicide mission for him. Nevertheless, he is determined to do his best to help Billy pull out of despair. Four years ago, his own situation was similar to this one and he came out of it. So, Billy should also be able to.

Grandpa decides to tell his story...

"Dear Billy, I know what you are going through. It's not easy.

I know you are thinking, "Oh come on! You don't understand," but trust me...I truly do understand. Not because I am older than you nor because I am expected to come here and play smart but because I went through somewhat similar situation four years ago, the night of the presidential election on Nov 8th, 2016. That night after Trump's victory...I felt devastated; I felt like killing myself.

I have been a lifelong Democrat, and I was at the convention center, ready to celebrate Hillary Clinton's victory, which was highly anticipated. I was with a group of friends there. We already had the champagne bottle out, ready to pop! And then, as the news of Trump's victory hit us, we just couldn't believe what we were hearing with our ears. We couldn't understand how's that possible. My eyes couldn't believe what I saw on the big screen! This must be a mistake. A terrible mistake! Something must have gone wrong. I felt like crying. I felt totally devastated. I felt totally unprepared for what was about to unfold that night. I collapsed on to the floor. Not just me but thousands of people in that convention center were at the verge of mental breakdown."

Initially, Billy was not keen to hear anything anyone has to say but there is a power in grandpa's storytelling. Five minutes down, Billy started getting curious.

Grandpa continued, "So, that night...I was not sure how to respond to what was going on. I felt totally lost. I sat there on the floor all night... horrible feelings torturing me. I looked around and most people were in a kind of similar situation. It's like mass hysteria. Many crying. Some holding their feelings in their hearts. Some people already left the place. Feeling all alone, I started walking. Where I don't know but soon, I found myself on the streets, middle of the night, chilly weather, no destination. I was totally dazed out. My mind was clouded with thoughts of despair and hopelessness. I was afraid, what's going to happen to this country that I love so much? What's going to happen to my grandkids? How can someone with such a low ethical standard become the President of the United States? How can someone so impulsive be in charge of the most powerful military on this earth? Are we all going to die in a nuclear war? My mind was going crazy. Fear was sending chills down my spine. I was feeling all confused. Suddenly, my thoughts were interrupted as I was pulled to the side by a stranger as I was oblivious of the fact that I was about to be hit by a truck. "Man! You are going to get yourself killed if you walk like that on the street."

"May be that's better" a voice inside my head made me reply sharply, "what's the point of living?" This situation is so horrible, and I definitely can't endure this for the next four years to come.

"You are out of your mind my friend" the stranger shouted. "Are you one of those miserable people coming out of that convention center? I saw many coming out deeply distressed and tearful." "Don't die here tonight. Go home and take some rest. You will feel better."

Grandpa paused here for a moment...lost in thought...looking out of the window recollecting the distant past.

"So, what happened?" asked Billy.

Grandpa resumed sighing heavily, "Went home that night with a heavy heart. Crazy thoughts passed through my mind. I was feeling suicidal. I know it's wrong. So, I called the suicide hotline, but it was busy...probably too many crazies out there that night making phone calls, seeking help."

"That made me feel even more desperate. What should I do now? How about I end my life right now? I have a gun at home, or I could simply slash my wrists with a knife. I have some sleeping pills too!"

Both Billy and Johnny are listening attentively...anxious to know what happened next.

Grandpa continued, "I would have died that night, if not for a friend that saved me. He lived across the street and noticed that I came home from the convention. He knew I was a staunch Democrat and thought I must be devastated. So, he came to check on me.

He learnt of my thoughts and the suicidal ideation, and he convinced me against doing anything crazy. He stayed with me that night and in the morning, we got some professional help. He took me to a doctor that he found very helpful for himself. This young doctor goes by the name Dr. Calm. **He advocates finding calm because calmness brings happiness and positive vibes into our life.**"

"So, how did you survive that episode? Was it easy to come out of it? What did Dr. Calm tell you?" asks Billy.

"That's going to be a long story. But, let me share with you some key points I learnt at that time and see if that helps."

Billy quietly nods his head.

Grandpa continues, "**There are four forces that help people come out of despair,** Dr. Calm told me."

"**The first one is Hope. Without hope there is nothing left. When a man loses hope, he loses everything.**"

"But sometimes there is no hope!" Billy exclaimed. "Take for example the current situation...there is so much negativity around. All I hear on TV is bad news. We as millennials have no hope. There is so much college debt. Even if we clear the debt, they are saying that the earth is going to drown pretty soon because of Global Warming with dialing back of environmental protection policies under the current administration. They are also saying that a war is going to break out with Iran, nuclear weapons will be used, and we will all die. That's really scary. Then why study, why pay college fee, and why care about anything. We are going to die anyway. You see there is no hope."

Grandpa smiles back, "Seems the situation is dire indeed, at least according to your view of this world. Do you mind if I share my world view?"

"Of course," Billy nods his head.

"Look, when I was about your age, we were in the middle of the World War II. Every day it felt as if I or someone else that I love was going to die. Every day was a doomsday! That continued for many years. Somehow, we survived." Grandpa continued, "It felt like we wouldn't, but we did. In fact, it's not just me but millions of people survived the world war. Not only we survived but the world has seen many innovations since then. But everyone was telling us that it was end of the world at that time. It turned out not to be true. Thank God!" smiles grandpa.

"You survived the world war! So, you think there is always hope?" for the first time a sense of hope is seen on Billy's face.

"Yes Billy. **There is always hope. Sometimes it may not feel like so when we are deep in the pit of misery but there is always hope for those who are willing to see the brighter side of life.**"

"Look we are nowhere near the magnitude of the problem the world was going through during the World Wars. Yes, I acknowledge that we have some major problems to solve in the world but it's nothing apocalyptic!

Our mind tends to project the worst possible outcomes when you are worried about any situation. It appears real to us in that moment but it's not real. Once you realize that, the dark clouds of despair in your mind dissolve, paving the path to light...the rays of hope. Once you see hope, things start getting better. Doesn't it make sense?" asked grandpa.

Billy, silently listening all this time, nods his head in understanding. "Yes, it makes sense. We take a given situation and somehow think about in our mind all the worst possible scenarios. And they may never happen. And **I have the choice not to imagine the worst possible scenario.** In fact, I can see some good possibilities of how my life can be better even with the current problems we are facing. **There are ways out of the problems we face. There is always a way out.** Is that what you are saying?"

"Exactly! Can't be better said."

"Ok let's say I have some hope now," says Billy smilingly, "What are the other forces that could help me out of this bad situation?"

"Great! The second force that helps us pull out of despair is FAITH."

"What do you mean by faith?"

"Faith simply means having confidence that all will be alright, no matter what your situation is. There are times when we as human beings do not know the answers to our problems, despite all information gathering and the analysis we do. During those times you got to believe in something. You got to believe in good. You got to believe that everything will be alright. That belief itself is Faith.

Some say have faith in God. Some others say have faith in the Universe or the Higher Power. I say, have faith in whatever that works for you! For me, I have gone through enough situations in life that **I know that in the end everything happens for good.** It turns out to be alright, even though during those moments I feel uncertain, fearful, and insecure. With experience, I have learnt to be faithful. **No one can teach you this. You have to develop your own faith.** But it is easy to develop if you start believing that everything will be alright no matter how dire your situation may look like. If you do not have enough personal experience in this area, then you can rely on others' experiences. There are enough stories of faith around.

Since the 2016 election night when I was ready to commit suicide, I came a long way. I had a wonderful time with my family past four years, I was able to sell my business and made lots of money that bought me freedom to travel around the world...in fact I had a blast of time the last eight years...even though I don't like the current President. You see, **who your President has very little to do with your personal happiness.** You still have a lot of choices to make and decide what you want to do with your life. Don't throw away your life so easily."

"Wow! It's amazing!!" Billy couldn't believe those words came out of his mouth...he was only deeply depressed just a little while ago. "So, **faith is essentially believing that all will be alright. And the more you believe in it the more things will be alright!** Hmmm, interesting. Never thought about it that way."

Grandpa continued, "Yes, nicely said. Remember, the Universe is full of abundance. It's infinite. There are so many resources out there. This Universe is not meant to be scarce. Scarcity has nothing to do with what is available out there...especially in America. Scarcity is a mentality. See how many natural resources and wealth is available to us. You are not in middle east or Africa where people are fighting and bombing each other every day and where there is deep civil unrest. You are in America...the land of freedom. Despite all the negative news constantly being played on TV, there is so much good in our country. There are so many good things out there. Go find them. They are there. Explore the world. Focus on the good and you will be alright. There is enough for everyone. It's all in your mind. Remember!"

Those words of encouragement acted like a tonic on Billy. He is totally charged now. He is up from his bed, sitting straight, and looking confident.

"Grandpa, I am so happy that you are here today helping me. Johnny, you are really fortunate to have a grandpa like this and thanks for bringing him to me today." Billy continued, "So grandpa, what are the other two forces that pull us out of despair?"

"Patience Billy Patience :)

Yes, the third force is Patience. Patience is a virtue. Sometimes no matter how smart we are, how much faith we may have, we will have to be patient.

Nature has its own timeline, despite what we want and how much hurry we are in to get things done. Losing patience only leads to frustration during those times. We need to abide by our time sometimes."

"Can you explain more about this?" inquires Billy.

"Sure. For example, let's say you sow seeds to grow an apple tree. No matter how many seeds you sow and how much water you pour, the apple seeds are going to take their time to grow into a tree and give you fruits. Just because you want fruits tomorrow, it doesn't happen urgently. It takes time for the apple seed to grow into a plant, then a tree, and then bear fruits. We must respect that process. That requires patience. **If you have enough patience, you can win the whole world. The one who lacks patience is often set to live a life of frustration. Choose how you want to live your life.**"

"But grandpa, sometimes we don't have the time to be patient" protested Billy.

"Yes Billy. That's true. Very true. In fact, painfully true. But what choice do we have my dear?

For example, many of the Democrats do not want President Trump to be in the office. They have been thinking about putting him in jail and preventing him from running for President again. See what happened...it only made Mr. Trump's resolve to win stronger and made him fight harder. The FBI probe, the Hush Money case, and many other investigative efforts aren't entirely fruitful. Are they? Ultimately, they will have to wait see what happens in the upcoming election. I wish the Democrats were wiser in making their choices. I believe they are blinded by their hatred and are not patient enough to let the democratic process to play out. In fact, by being impatient they may be inadvertently facilitating Mr. Trump winning the 2024 election."

"Anyway, the point is when you lose patience and act frustrated, your situation gets worse instead of getting resolved. So, be wise and be patient. It will ultimately pay off."

"How? Can you help apply what you said to my situation?"

"Don't you think you have been impatient? You are just in your early 20s. You barely got into college, and you have a long life ahead and a great career possibly, if you study well. But you got impatient with yourself and tried to commit suicide. You just imagined in your mind the worse possible scenarios, but you failed to realize that those bad scenarios are more a projection of your mind rather than the reality. The reality is always different than what you imagine. You could have taken your parents or friends' help to talk it out and resolve the situation rather than harming yourself my dear.

Remember, you don't have any situation that is worse than the innocent kids dying of bombing in Israel-Hamas war? Gang warfare and violence have transformed parts of Central America into some of the most dangerous places on earth. Thousands of parents have fled with their families and, in many cases, children have made the perilous journey alone. These unaccompanied children are some of the world's most vulnerable **refugees**. Did you ever think about the kids born in terrorism and grew up with no mother, no father, and are constantly being used for Jihad against their will?

You see my dear, there are far worse things in this world. When you see that, you suddenly realize that your situation is not bad at all. It's just a matter of perspective! You have a bright life ahead. It's all up to you how you use your talents. **Be patient with yourself and let things play out. Take one step at a time...whatever it is. And ultimately everything will be alright.** Take one day at a time. Enjoy every moment. Plan your career properly, expect obstacles, expect failures, but be ready to overcome them too. And you will be alright."

Billy and Johnny are listening attentively. Grandpa continues...

"Don't make the President and the problems of the world determine your happiness. They have only a small role in determining your destiny. **90% of your destiny depends on the decisions you make in your day-to-day life rather than what the President is doing in the Oval office.** Remember, even the worst Presidency is only going to last 4 years or may be 8 years. Your life span is possibly 80 years. So, 4-8 years is a short time compared to your life span. Keep marching forward. Never lose your hope. Always have faith. Be patient. And you will be fine."

By this time, Billy is totally feeling well and is enthusiastic to learn more, "So, what's the fourth force?"

"Endurance. We all need to develop strength and endurance. Life is a series of challenges. With each challenge make sure you become stronger and better. **Life is not a sprint. It's a marathon.** To run a marathon, a short burst of energy is not enough. You need to develop endurance. You develop endurance by withstanding trials and not giving up. **You develop endurance by getting up every time you fall down, by not letting failure deter you from moving forward and succeeding in life.** Develop that power of endurance.

Combine these four forces and despair will never come close to you. You will become invincible to the lashes of fate!"

Billy is totally relaxed, his face lit with newfound optimism, ready to jump out of the bed and roll.

The nurse who just walked in, found this all very strange. She couldn't figure out how this kid who was feeling suicidal and totally hopeless during her last visit an hour ago, now cheerful. She quickly runs to the doctor, asking him to order a urine drug screen to see if we sneaked in any illegal drugs to Billy to give him a high!!

Meanwhile Billy's parents return from lunch, and they are equally astounded to see their son happy. They are curious about what happened exactly but didn't ask us how. I am sure they will ask Billy after we leave. With that, grandpa and I decided to move on and went back home to have some nice fresh homemade pasta.

Chapter 5
Election Stress is Created from Within

**Grandpa helps Johnny understand how
we humans suffer from overthinking.**

Grandpa, "I know that Billy has turned around. That's a great thing. But will he continue to stay hopeful?"

"Well, if he doesn't go back to the old ways of thinking, he will be alright. We suffer more than what we need to because we misuse our thinking."

"What do you mean by that grandpa?" asks Johnny.

"It means that **we create suffering through our own thinking. We magnify our suffering by using our thinking against ourselves.**"

"Hmmm. That's interesting. Tell me more."

"**Most stress comes from our thinking of the situation rather than the situation itself. Situations happen outside, but stress happens inside.**

How stressed we are, depends on how much we are stuck in our thinking.

Let's say your boss scolded you. You feel bad about it. It's normal to feel bad at that time. But most people continue to feel bad about it for weeks and months after the incident happens. They continue to stress about it because they keep thinking about the incident, even though their boss has long forgotten about it. Their mind is stuck thinking about it, like a CD that is stuck playing the same song. That's how we create chronic stress in our lives.

Once the incident is over, the boss has very little to do with the stress you feel, unless he continues to instigate you.

Chronic stress results from repetitive, dysfunctional thinking about an incident that's no longer present. Sometimes it's about an event that happened in the past and sometimes it's about the future that's not yet here. Most chronic stress results either from the memory of past traumatic events or imagination of a fearful future."

"Are you saying all stress results from our thinking, and we don't need to stress at all?" asks Johnny.

"To answer that question, I need to explain you the difference between acute stress and chronic stress.

Let me share with you a story that Dr. Calm often recites to make this distinction.

Imagine a zebra is being hunted down by a lion in Africa. Being hunted triggers an acute stress response in the zebra. Her heart races, pumps blood faster, lungs breathe rapidly, the energy stores are mobilized in her body so that she could run faster and escape from the lion. Hopefully the zebra is lucky enough to escape. After the zebra escapes, she comes to its normal state of being in 30-40 minutes. The acute stress response dissipates. She joins the herd, grazes, and moves along. This acute stress response is normal and physiological. **When we face a threat it's normal to feel acutely stressed.**

Now, imagine yourself in the same situation as the zebra. Let's say you went on an African Safari trip. Despite the tour guide's warning, you strayed away from the group and encountered a lion, barely 20 feet away. You freeze. You start sweating, your heart racing, feeling palpitations, and you can't think straight. The lion smells your fear. Takes a step forward, ready to attack you. You almost faint. Can't even move. You close your eyes, ready to be attacked by the lion any minute!

Then comes a banging sound from behind you...the tour guide with his rifle scares away the lion. He finds you limp with no energy, your whole-body trembling. He takes you back to the tour bus. After an hour, finally, you stop sweating and shaking, coming back to your senses.

A bunch of tourists gather around you, curious about your 'safari experience'. Though your body has calmed down, your mind has not. You are still thinking about the lion. You feel terrible about this whole 'lion' situation you went through. You start cursing the lion. You start telling others how terrible this lion is and all the lions must be locked up and that a safari tour is not a good idea as long as lions are roaming around. **You go** on narrating this terrible story of yours the whole day and you wonder why you continue to feel worse.

Then you go back to your hotel and that night you don't sleep well. You wake up in the middle of the night screaming and dreaming that the lion is attacking you. Tossing and turning, unable to sleep, you call your family 10,000 miles away and tell them the terrible story, to their dismay. By morning, you feel so irritable and tired that you cancel your tour for that day. Though it was your lifelong dream to go on an African Safari Tour, you are not enjoying it anymore. You cancel the trip altogether to go back to your home country. Back home, you continue to tell this story whenever you get a chance. **Three months later, you continue to have nightmares about the lion attacking you. Now, you got Post-Traumatic Stress Disorder (PTSD).**

Johnny, you see what the problem is here?

You continue to stress about an event that is no longer present. The lion has long forgotten you, but you haven't forgotten the lion. That's the problem.

That's the difference between the zebra who forgot the lion after an hour vs. a human being who continued to brood over it for months, misusing his power of thinking. That's how we create chronic psychological stress in our lives...by repetitively thinking about stuff that happened in the past and sometimes, even worse, thinking about stuff that hasn't happened yet!" finishes grandpa.

"Wow! That's an amazing story to demonstrate that **we use our thinking against ourselves and create suffering simply by repeating our thoughts.**"

"Yes, my dear grandson. And **the unfortunate thing is that we don't even realize that we are doing it to ourselves.** It's because no one ever teaches us this stuff. But, once I realized that I am creating my own stress, using my own thinking against myself, I stopped doing it.

Initially, it was hard because of bad habits. But, with time, I succeeded in not thinking about stuff all the time. That liberated my mind from a lot of stress.

And you know what's even more exciting? I realized that **anything appears real only as long as we think about it.** If you could really stop thinking about all the negative stuff, there are no words to explain the mental freedom you experience. You feel so much better about everything in life. You start seeing good in everything around you, because your mind is not anymore preoccupied with the bad stuff. More on this later."

"Thanks for sharing this grandpa. It's quite a revelation for me and I will try to implement this in my life starting today. But can you explain me how this pertains to Trump and the upcoming elections? Many people I know are worried what's going to happen in the upcoming 2020 elections. Is Trump going to win again? What if he gets reelected?"

"You think too much about all this stuff Johnny and that's the reason your brain feels like exploding!" exclaims grandpa. "I have friends who don't think about this at all, and they don't feel election stress, even though a lot is happening out there. I want you to know that it's possible not to be stressed about the elections."

Johnny nods his head but still not completely convinced that it is possible to be free of election stress.

Noticing that, grandpa chuckles, "Alright, let's discuss Trump, Biden, and elections a little bit. You ready for it?

Look Johnny, to evade election stress, the first thing that I want you to remember is, **most stress we face in this modern world is psychological.** Today, we human beings unlike our ancestors who used to live in the wild, rarely face physical threats like a lion or bear hunting us down. You may say what about physical threats like getting mugged or being physically abused by someone. Of course, those are real threats and must be fought and handled appropriately. Even when there are no physical threats, people are stressed for different reasons, mostly **psychological.** It's about what your boss said last week, how terrible your colleagues are, why does your spouse always have to argue with you, why are you not as cool as your Facebook friends or what's the election news this morning...you get the idea...**we stress ourselves by thinking about stuff rather than being under some kind of physical threat!**"

Johnny, listening to all this carefully, lost deep in thought, asks, "So, you are saying that **most stress we feel in our lives is because of our thinking about the situation rather than the situation itself.** That means whether it is elections or something else, we are stressed about it because of our constant thinking about it, being exposed to the news, discussions on social media, and arguing with friends and family, rather than what is going on out there. It has nothing to do with what's going on out there. Is that what you are saying?"

"Absolutely! That's awesome Johnny, the way you have put it. That's true. But I wouldn't say that stress has nothing to do with what's going on out there. Obviously, our environment and the events happening around us impact us. That said, **there are always things happening out there. It is up to us whether we want them to affect us or not.**

Stress is a choice. We can decide whether to get stressed out or not, especially amid constant turmoil. That is what I realized when I was going through an awful amount of anxiety during the last election.

At that time, I learnt that **'THE TRUTH' of what's really happening out there in Washington DC, never reaches us untainted.** It's mired. The information we get goes through multiple layers...the journalist who gathers the information, the way the news channels filter them based on their political affiliations, how the newsreaders deliver the message to appeal to their audience, the kind of show you are watching, and more. Also, remember that the editors and producers of the TV/Radio show may modify the material to their liking. Keep in mind that the programs on TV and radio are made to entertain audience and to obtain great ratings. So many factors affect the information we receive through media. So many changes happen before the news is delivered to us, the consumer.

When you watch Fox News, you get a different perspective about Trump and Biden when compared to CNN's view of them. Who should I believe? What is the Truth? **How do I discern Truth from false propaganda?** I honestly don't know what's the **Truth**. Then why should I stress about it? Is it worth stressing and jeopardizing my health? I don't think so.

Even when you got all your facts right, I don't see how it helps us to internalize horrible news and stress about it.

If you could do something to change the outcomes of the politics and the policies made by the politicians, do it. Be proactive about it. Advocate for the right things to be done. But just don't sit there and panic about the problems. Don't brood over them. Don't spread negativity. Take positive action. But that's not what I see. Most people just sit there and worry. That doesn't help them. So, let go of the negativity.

Remember, what's happening in our house is more important than what's going on in the white house.

Yes, the policies made by the politicians will have some effect on our lives. But a majority of our destiny depends on our day to day decisions on how we conduct ourselves. No President or political party is going to change your life drastically. You need to be smart, work hard, and calmly do what you need to succeed in life. Those people who do that will do well in life regardless.

Yes, you may say that some people's lives change overnight depending on who wins in the upcoming elections. But you are not a congressman, you are not a senator, you are not a journalist reporting the news every day, and you are not anywhere near Washington DC. For a vast majority of people like you and me, **our destiny depends more on what we do and how we conduct ourselves every day in our lives.** That's an undebatable Truth! And that we must focus upon!" concludes grandpa.

It's late at night. They both didn't notice how much time has lapsed since they began the discussion. Johnny is deeply lost in thought, thinking about all that happened just in one day. He is feeling better. Much has changed in just one day. Johnny goes to sleep with a sense of lightness in his heart.

Chapter 6
The Future Is Not as Dire as You Think

Grandpa counsels Johnny to be informed about the presidential candidates, make a choice, but don't stress over the elections.

The next morning, Johnny wakes up refreshed and peaceful. He hasn't slept well for months, owing to the nonstop worrying about the elections; all that came to a halt last night. But, as soon as he woke up, he notices those worried thoughts about the future started bothering him again. He slowly walks to the living room and notices that grandpa is already awake and making breakfast. He wishes good morning and joins him.

"Oh! You are awake!! Nice. Come on, let's have some nice breakfast. You didn't eat much last evening. By the way, how did you sleep last night?" inquires grandpa.

"Slept well, in fact very well. Something changed in me last night. I felt a sense of calm. But as soon as I woke up and saw the news about impeachments proceedings, the thoughts about the upcoming election started bothering me. Hugh! I don't know what's going to happen. I am worried about it."

"Got it Johnny. I know you are worried and there is a reason for it. You are not alone. Many people I know are imagining a fearful future about the upcoming 2020 elections. I see both Democrats and Republicans stressed out, though for different reasons.

Republicans are worried whether Trump is going to be elected or not and what the Democrats are conspiring to put him in jail. They are constantly looking for ways to undermine Trump. They are extremely worried that if Democrats win again, the recession will continue, the immigration crisis persists, and the Nation's future is going to spiral down.

However, most Democrats' thinking is centered around what could go wrong if Trump wins this time.

Will our nation survive a second term of the Trump Presidency?

"Is Trump going to do things to dismantle the current political structure so that he can continue on as the supreme ruler...like China's Xi Jinping? Is there going to be a dictatorship in the United States? Is he going to take revenge on Democrats for all the probes and court cases laid against him.

Remember, Trump really loved the idea when China has approved the

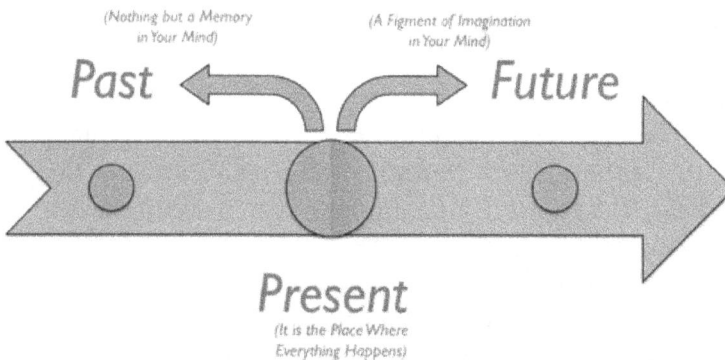

removal of the two-term limit on the presidency, effectively allowing Xi Jinping to remain in power for life."

According to CNN, in March 2018, Trump said to the cheering and applauding supporters,

"Look, the Chinese President was able to do that. I think it's great. Maybe we'll have to give that a shot someday!"

So, what would happen if Trump wins in 2024? Will White Supremacy reign? What's the fate of all the immigrants? What will happen to our court system? Will there be a refugee crisis and kids be separated from parents again? Will Trump collude with Russia, China, and other foreign powers? Is there a chance that Trump will push the boundaries of presidential power to his advantage? Will there be more scandals? Will a Civil War breakout? Will the humankind survive at all, in light of accelerated Global warming?

These are some serious questions, that many of my Democrat friends are concerned about."

Grandpa pauses for a moment.

Johnny was listening intently to what grandpa has been saying. He's feeling unsettled, to put it lightly, thinking about all the bad possibilities if Trump wins again.

Grandpa continues, "So, how do you feel?"

"Terrible and depressed! We discuss all this stuff on social media" promptly replies Johnny. "The prospect doesn't look good at all."

Grandpa continues, "Of course, you feel depressed as you think about all this! We just ran down a list of the most horrible prospects in the future. But are you sure that all this is going to happen in the future, or it is just our wild imagination?"

"I don't know" replies Johnny.

Grandpa chuckles, **"Past is a memory, future is a figment of your imagination, and present is the only place where everything happens."**

The truth is, none of that is happening at this moment! Those things may never happen. Who knows? Then why imagine a terrible future?

There is another important point we need to note here Johnny – our mind has the capability to create endless number of questions and possibilities. **If we let our mind wander, it can create a havoc by imagining all the worst possible scenarios. Our mind needs restraint and proper guidance.**

The future is not here yet. Lot of these questions that are circulating around, are simply a creation of our fearful minds.

Between now and the election day in November 2024, anything can happen. May be Trump will win. Maybe Biden will. Who knows? All you can do is to learn the best about each of the candidates running for the President, advocate for the one you choose, and vote. For most normal people like you and me, that's the best course of action to take. Anything beyond, is not in our control. There is no point stressing about it because it is not going to help. If you are stressed enough, you can jeopardize your health, fight with your friends and family, and live a miserable life. I personally think that's not worth it."

"I agree that the elections are not worth stressing about, grandpa. Many of my friends are fighting with each other, some broke up with their girlfriends, one of my professors got admitted to the hospital because of high anxiety and a mini-heart attack, my mom and dad fight at home every day over politics...too much going on already. I just can't imagine what will happen as we inch closer to the election day."

Grandpa nods his head and continues, "I think it's unwise to be stressed over the elections. **Aren't elections controlled by big money? 'We the people' – are we really in control of our democracy?**

We all know that the elections are controlled by big corporations, big media, and big lobbyists. There is a hypothesis out there that the election results are already bought out and all this noise about elections is just a drama. The last two times, the candidate with the most popular votes didn't win and some people say that the electoral votes were bought out!

We think we are in control of electing our leaders by voting but it is a few rich people who ultimately decide the fate of the nation. The political system is already bought out. The economics of the nation is driven by a few multibillion-dollar companies. The media is controlled by a handful of networks. Whatever they want to propagate, they can effectively do so.

When you look at all this, you may start to wonder, "Where is democracy?" Is it an illusion? We the people, do we have really any control? For most part aren't we just doing what the big companies want us to do?

Apple gives you a 100-page disclaimer before you buy an iPhone but who can read and understand all that legal jargon. Yet, you sign it. Isn't it? Where is legal help for the common man?

AT&T won't discount you any money because you have dropped calls and poor network at your home. You still have to pay them every month the same fee as someone who lives in areas with excellent coverage. Where is justice?

The cable networks monopolize the entertainment industry and you have to pay them whatever they charge if you want access to TV programs. Where is free choice?

Isn't everything controlled by a few big companies and we just go along with them?

Why is that so much tobacco and alcohol are being sold even though many people die of cancer and cirrhosis every year? Where is proper regulation?

You have illegal immigrants coming in, but half of our politicians are opposing the policies to have strict border control. The other day, I was speaking with a border patrol agent, a neighbor of mine and he tells me horrible stories about the drug cartels. He tells me that in his 20 years of experience, neither the Republicans nor the Democrats wanted to take any decisive action on border control because of political and selfish reasons.

You see, there are many theories out there. And I don't know for sure if they are right or wrong. All I can do is examine what's going on in my vicinity to the best of my ability. All I can control is, my thoughts and actions. If I could do that, there are 90% chances that I am going to do alright in my life. **When it comes to elections, many things are beyond our control, but our happiness is still under our control.**

Take your destiny into your hands Johnny. Don't leave it to the unknown possibilities of the future. Stay grounded. Be strong. Do what you got to do to excel in your life, both professionally and personally. That will take you a long way in leading a successful life.

If everyone takes responsibility for their own happiness, most of the problems we face in this world disappear. But the selfishness and laziness that plague the human minds is the greatest hindrance for individual progress than which political party is going to prevail over the next four years.

Remember, many politicians and Presidents changed their terms over the past many decades, but the life of common man hasn't changed drastically. The only way to change our lives drastically is to take our destiny into our hands. Most successful people will vouch for this truth."

Johnny was carefully listening "So, you are urging me to just do my duty and not worry too much about the results."

"Exactly! And let me share with you an encouraging fact – **The worst possible situations we think never come to pass by, most of the times**" smiles grandpa reassuringly with a twinkle in his eyes, "**Our minds tend to project a fearful future, but it is often not as dire as we think!**"

Feeling relieved, Johnny sits back and relaxes in the chair, thinking "**A fearful future is an imagination of my mind, and I shouldn't fall for it.**"

Grandpa continues, "Let's take your friend Billy for example. His mind was constantly creating the worst possible scenarios about the future. Isn't it? What if Trump wins? What if he never makes enough money to clear his college debt? What if Global Warming drowns the city he lives in? Then what's the point of living? Any way I am miserable, and I am going to die!

Because he thought he was in the worst possible situation and felt that there was absolutely no way out of it, he attempted suicide."

"But, let me ask you. Is it true that Billy was facing the worst possible situation with no solutions at all?"

Johnny thinks for a moment and replies, "I don't think so. We just showed him a solution. He just came out of it."

"You are right. Then why did he feel so desperate? Because, for him it appeared very real, though for us it is not. **Your reality depends on the thoughts you think.** He was thinking negative thoughts and projecting a horrible future in his mind, and he came to believe it. He felt hopeless. He went into total despair."

"Wait, wait grandpa. I see something. Hold on. Hold on. Oh, got it! I see it! I see it!!" exclaims Johnny. *"Whatever thoughts are running through my mind, that's what is creating my reality. Once those thoughts pass by, that reality drops away and will be replaced by something else based on my next thoughts.* **So, thoughts create transient realities and whatever thoughts I focus on, that becomes my reality.**

It's like changing TV channels. If I am watching a horror movie on TV, I feel horrified. But, if I am watching a feel-good movie, I feel upbeat. So, are you saying that the remote control to our life is in our hands? I mean, I can switch channels in my mind at will, by changing what I am thinking and that's how I create the reality of my life? So, I don't have to be stuck thinking about Trump, just because some news channel talks about him all day? Eureka! I am on to something here!" says Johnny, all excited.

He continues, "So, I am in control of my life? **I can choose what to think or not, no matter what other people are saying or thinking about me.** So, it ultimately doesn't matter what's going on around you. If people are saying bad things, you don't have to listen to them. Whatever they are saying is just their thinking about me but actually it's not me. It's their reality and not mine. If they are living in a horrible reality, it's their choice but I don't have to buy into it."

"Now I see why Billy was so desperate and attempted a suicide. He was living in a horrible reality in his mind, when actually he is leading a pretty comfortable life. There are so many young people out there with much worse prospect than Billy. They don't have food to eat, no water to drink, no medicine if they get sick, and are being recruited to become terrorists at a young age before they know what they are doing. Billy's situation is nowhere close to theirs.

Billy has rich parents. He is in college. He is in America with lots of resources. He got good grades. I mean there is so much good stuff in his life, but he failed to notice it because he was too focused on what he doesn't have and what can go wrong. He was stuck thinking about all the problems. Soon, he found himself in despair.

Oh, I see! His mind tricked him to believe that he is in the worst possible situation, when in reality he is not!" exclaims Johnny.

"**Exactly! You can have everything in the world and yet feel hopeless if you focus on what you don't have.**

So, he was just trapped in his thinking that there was no way out, until we showed him a way out. That's how our mind tricks us into a corner and makes us feel hopeless. That's how most problems in life are."

For Every Problem, There Is A Solution

"Yes grandpa, that I see, but don't we have problems to solve and situations to resolve in life?"

"Of course, we all have problems to solve. We don't ignore them. We do our best to solve them. That doesn't mean that we brood over them. **Most people fail to solve their problems because they brood over them rather than taking the time to solve them!**"

There are always solutions to our problems. Just because we don't see them right now, it doesn't mean they are not existent. May be someone else has the solution. May be if we give enough time, we will find the solution. Maybe it requires a different way of thinking about it. Right?"

Like Albert Einstein said, "The problems we created cannot be solved at the same level of thinking they were created.

"But there are problems out there that have no solution! Isn't it, grandpa?"

"In your mind, yes! But maybe **there are solutions out there that you just do not know yet! Just because you don't have the solution, it doesn't mean there is no solution at all!** It's a matter of staying hopeful, having faith, and patiently continuing to do your best that matters. That's how you move forward in life...one step at a time and see where it takes us. Maintain an attitude of curiosity rather than worrying at every turn of life. Then life becomes an exciting journey!"

"But, even after all that you may not find solutions!"

"Sometimes that's true. But what are you going to do about it? If you just don't find what you want, does it mean that life is not worth living? No! What about all the other things that are going well for you? Shouldn't you be grateful for them?

"If you are always dependent on something external to happen for you to feel happy, then you got the wrong concept of happiness. It's just an illusion that you got to achieve something, so that you could feel happy. Your happiness lies within. When people realize that, they will be less worried about what's going to happen. You will be happy no matter what! Learn to be happy no matter who your President is and then all this election frenzy is not going to bother you so much. More on that later though, my dear grandson. It's time for lunch."

"That sounds interesting. My happiness comes from within. Okay. Will wait to hear more about it later."

Chapter 7
Should We Even Care
Who Gets Elected?

Grandpa reveals the three prescriptions from Dr. Calm to maintain sanity during the election cycle.

Johnny and grandpa take off for lunch. They drive to a nice local restaurant. Grandpa says that he goes there often. The food is great and the people who serve at the restaurant are fabulous. They are kind and of helping nature. As they order their favorite food and waiting for it, grandpa notices a long-time acquaintance approaching him. He quickly whispers in Johnny's ears, watch carefully what happens...

"Hey Drew! How are you doing? Good to see you" wishes grandpa.

Drew is a tall and hefty middle-aged man with a beard, observes Johnny.

"I am doing good my friend. How are you doing? Who is this young man next to you?"

"This is my grandson, Johnny. He just came here to visit me for this weekend. We came down for lunch. So, what's up with you? What's new?"

"You know, not really much. The election season is up again, and I am quite worried what's going to happen. Did you see all that commotion about possible Trump conviction on TV last night? It's terrible, isn't it? All those 'do good for nothing' Democrats hate Trump. They are trying to convict Trump from day one of Biden taking the office. I mean, that's terrible. Give him a break. These Democrats are not letting him be at peace. In the past, they failed to prove that there is any collusion with Russia after the Mueller's team spent millions of dollars. Mueller's team was full of attorneys that support Democrats and still they couldn't prove it. Now, this conviction stuff is going to backfire also. It's going to be bad for Democrats in the upcoming elections.

I mean, when Trump was the president, the economy was doing so good and businesses were booming. Job growth was great. I felt good about where the nation was going under Trump. Yes, he has his eccentricities, but he got the job done, I think! No one had the guts to implement the border control and he was doing it. No one had the courage to go on a trade war with China, for manipulating the currency for decades and Trump went after China. I think he was right in asking the NATO allies to pay for their part. He was able to meet with North Korean dictator Kim Jong Un and there was some progress there. I mean, lots of good things happened when Trump was our President. He kept most of his promises, unlike the regular politicians. But now I am worried if they are going to put him in jail. I am worried if he is going to win or not. What do you say?"

Johnny feels like throwing up, listening to all that Drew just said. How can someone like Trump so much? This guy seems to Love Trump!! That's crazy. Johnny feels like getting up and walking away but grandpa's sitting next to him. He kept quiet, watching what grandpa is going to say.

Grandpa replies, "That's right drew. I think our economy was doing good and we made some progress for sure. By the way, do you want to sit down and join us for lunch?"

"No, my friend. I must go back to work. I quickly stopped by here to grab some coffee. Let's catch up some other time. Always pleasure to see you" and with that, Drew took off from there.

And Johnny sighed with sense of great relief. "Thank God! I didn't have to sit down with him for lunch. My head would have exploded listening to his adulation of Trump. He must be a terrible guy like Trump."

Grandpa breaks out in laughter, "Oh Johnny! Take it easy. Drew is a good guy. He works hard. He is a self-made man. I know him since he was a teenager. He went through a lot of trouble in life and never gave up. He overcame one obstacle after another, patiently and diligently building his career. He has one kid, but he adopted a couple of orphans to give them a good life."

"Oh! That's nice of him. Sorry, didn't realize that he is such a nice man.

Then how can he be a Trump supporter?"

"You see Johnny, **we can't judge people based on their political affiliations. Everyone has the right to their perspective.** Just because someone has a different perspective than ours, we don't hate them. If Drew listened to your rant about Trump yesterday, he would have gone totally ballistic. How would you feel if he judges you by your love for Democrats?" smilingly says grandpa. "Aren't you a nice guy and you still dislike Trump? Then why can't Drew be a nice man who dislikes Democrats? In life, there are different people with different perspectives and different likings. We need to respect them all for who they are. Some media outlets tend to demonize certain groups of people. **Just because someone is wearing a MAGA (Make America Great Again) hat and is a Trump supporter, it doesn't mean they are bad people.** We got be careful not to judge people and label them just based on their appearance or their political inclinations. We truly need to understand people before we judge them. Now, let's finish our lunch, the food is getting cold. Can't wait to have a bite!"

Johnny and grandpa finish their lunch at leisure and slowly drive back home. Grandpa excuses himself for the rest of the afternoon, "Johnny, I got to do some gardening work this afternoon. Why don't you relax a little bit?"

"Sure grandpa. Thanks for the delicious lunch. Will see you later this evening."

It's early evening. Johnny was sitting there in the patio, gazing into the sky, reminiscing and trying to digest all that he has learnt the past two days. He is feeling so relaxed and confident, knowing that his destiny depends more on his day-to-day decisions than who his President is. He has a choice, whether to live happily no matter who wins in the upcoming elections vs. be miserable. He would rather choose to be happy. There is no need to empower Trump, Biden, or any politician to make his life miserable. His happiness lies within.

That evening, after a long process of thinking back and forth, contemplating what all he has learnt, Johnny finally feels content and confident that no matter who the president is, he is going to be happy and he decides his future, not someone else. He doesn't care anymore who wins.

But with that decision, a new question arises in him "If I can be happy no matter who the President is, then should I even care about the elections, the candidates, and who gets elected? Should I even vote? Should I even participate in any of the rallies, activities, and campaigns? He has been always active in such events from a very young age. But I don't want to bother Grandpa at this time. He has already spent most of his weekend dealing with me, my friend, and his parents. I will ask him first thing in the morning," thinking all that Johnny dozes off.

Next day at breakfast, he poses the question to grandpa, should we even care who gets elected? Grandpa bursts into an uncontrollable laughter... making Johnny even more perplexed. Trying to control his laughter he explains, "**Of course you should care who gets elected. You should vote. You should participate in all the activities you would like to. Just make sure you don't get pulled into the political turmoil, that's all.**"

Johnny asks, "Is that even possible?"

"Of course, it is possible," replies grandpa "though initially it may be difficult."

"Here are the three prescriptions from Dr. Calm that have been helping me tremendously to maintain my sanity during the election cycle.

1. Prioritize peace of mind above all: If there is an activity that could pull you apart and rob you of peace, then don't do it. Carefully choose what you want to do.

2. Take in all the information with a grain of salt: Be wise in discerning how much truth is there in what you hear and see in the news and social media.

3. Maintain strict media ration: Select a few media outlets whether TV/Radio/Magazines that you like and limit the amount of time you spend on them to less than 30 min a day. Do not participate in any negative social media campaigns/posts.

Grandpa goes on to expand on them:

1. Prioritize Peace of Mind Above All: If there is an activity that could pull you apart and rob you of peace, don't do it.

"What do you mean by that grandpa?" inquires Johnny curiously.

"Do you have a calendar that you use? Tell me what your priorities are for the next week or two."

"Johnny opens his google calendar app and quickly replies, alright, I have an assignment to submit for a course that I am taking in college. Then, I have a couple of friends coming in to visit me and we are planning to go hiking. Then, I have a local event where one of the Presidential candidates will be giving a speech. I have my birthday coming up and need to do some preparations. Those are the big ones and there are a few other little things to be done."

"That all sounds good Johnny. But I see a problem there."

"What's it? asks Johnny surprisingly.

"I don't see anything there that prioritizes peace of mind."

"What? How do you do that?" asks Johnny.

"Well, it's more a mindset issue than 'doing it' issue. Did you ever wonder why most people lack peace of mind in their lives?

It's because it's never a priority to them. People prioritize making money, doing work, meeting family and friends, watching TV, and going to movies etc. but never prioritize 'finding peace'. That's the reason they never find it.

For example, if you want to ace in exams, you got to prioritize studying and honing your test taking skills. Right? If you want to get ahead in career, you got to prioritize work. The same way, **if you want to stay peaceful in your life, you got to prioritize it**. Most people never prioritize it and so they never find it. All of a sudden when things are going wrong and they want peace in their lives, they don't know how to find it. That's the reason so many people are leading miserable lives."

"Hmmm! That's interesting. I never heard this concept. So, what do we do for that?"

"You could set up some quiet time each day. You could meditate, practice relaxing your mind, or read books that help you find peace. There are many things one could do. But it is not so much about doing. It is about recognizing that peace of mind is an entity to be prioritized like anything else.

But, in our modern society, for most people 'PEACE OF MIND' is not a priority. We didn't grow up thinking about it that way.

And you can't prioritize anything in life unless you think it's important. Right?

Most people don't realize that being at peace is probably the most important thing that matters.

Only if a person is calm and peaceful, he can lead a life of balance. When your mind is at peace you make better decisions in life, you perform optimally at work, and you are more energetic and healthier. Peaceful people are kind, loving, and helpful.

You may have name, fame, money, power, possessions, and more but

all that doesn't matter if you lack peace. What's the point if you are unhappy and miserable, despite having all the material things? How many people on their death bed wish that they should have spent more time saving their own souls? Too many!

There are celebrities, doctors, lawyers, and millionaires out there who have everything else except that they are so stressed and depressed that they don't know what to do. Ultimately, all the stress they face leads to major health problems, or they get into drugs, become suicidal, end up with broken relationships, or something else that's not good for them.

You see, **when a person is not peaceful and happy for a long time, it leads to unnecessary complications in life.** To avoid them, we all must prioritize our peace of mind and happiness first. That's the number one recommendation above all.

Especially, this election season, people tend to forget this. They start fighting with friends or family arguing about politics. I have seen broken relationships because of political rifts. One of my colleague's teenage daughter was told by her grandmother to not to attend the Christmas party because she supported Trump. That's awful. Is your granddaughter not entitled to her opinion? Isn't getting along with your grand daughter and her happiness more important than what's happening out there in Washington DC?

When people lose sight of what is really important in life, they do all sorts of things that jeopardize their wellbeing.

So, make sure you prioritize your peace of mind throughout this election season. If there is a rally where people are violent and disruptive, don't be part of it. If there is a social media firestorm spreading negativity, don't be part of it. Simply ask yourself, "If I do this, will it rob me of peace. If the answer is yes, don't do it."

Johnny was listening carefully.

Grandpa continues, "The second prescription I was given by Dr. Cam is...

2. Take in All the Information with a Grain of Salt: Be wise in discerning how much truth is there in what you see in the news and on social media.

The media tends to blow up things way out of proportion. According to them, the **sky is always falling.** It has been like that since my childhood. So, I don't take the information presented to me on TV seriously. I see it more as an entertainment. The truth is, we are not doing that bad as a nation. May be there are disagreements between Democrats and Republicans but still at the end of the day, we are doing fine.

What's happening in the middle east where some people don't have food to eat, no water to drink, and being bombed upon constantly is much worse than we have ever been in our lives. We are not refugees in crisis. We aren't experiencing any of the atrocities the third world countries are facing, where infants are dying due to lack of nutrition and adults are dying because they can't afford medications that only cost a few dollars. Most Americans live a comfortable life. Honestly, there shouldn't be much to complain, except for our own attitude towards life.

How bad your situation is simply a mental construct, created by your thinking influenced by the kind of information you are constantly getting. Your brain is only as

good as the information it receives. It's up to you to decide what kind of information you are going to let in. That decides the outlook you have about everything in life.

Be wise and avoid being drawn into media sensationalism. It's their duty to find exciting information and draw people into watching their channel. That's how they make money and survive financially. **It's your duty to guard your mind from unnecessary information, to survive the election stress.**

Use your discretion when watching news. Choose your channels wisely. One of my colleagues said recently, **"If you don't watch the news, you are uninformed. If you watch it, you are misinformed."** That's so true. So, **be like a wise ant that differentiates sugar crystals from sand.** Carefully discern good from bad and consume only things that are good for you. Everything media says, take it with a pinch of salt. See how much truth is in there. If you aren't sure about it, discard it. Keep your mind free of prejudice."

"But is it possible to really discern the truth watching the news on TV or reading newspapers? I feel like they are so biased. On Fox News, they portray Trump as an angel. On CNN and MSNBC, he is almost like a devil. Johnny expresses his doubt.

"That's the biggest problem we have in our media Johnny. Our media has lost objectivity. No person is always wrong. No person is 100% bad, including Trump. But, **if you look at liberal media outlets, Trump is never** right, no matter what he does. That's just not possible. People need to realize that. They need to hold media responsible when they are being biased.

For example, there are some things Trump did that are laudable. Before Trump, ISIS was beheading people almost every other day. The world leadership, including USA failed terribly in controlling ISIS. After Trump came in, we didn't see any of that. He kept his promise that he will crack down on ISIS. But the liberal media didn't give him or his administration much credit. No one can deny that we were doing well economically, the stock market was at an all-time high, and the job growth was good if not the best. Again, liberal media didn't give him enough credit.

The same is true for conservative media. Even when Trump's administration separated little children from their parents in refugee camps, some conservative media turned blind eye to it. Even when Trump badmouths his fellow Americans, he is not being held accountable by most conservative media. Trump's behavior as a President was not something most Americans approved of no matter what his policies were. But that is Trump. **Americans knew who he was for years and still they voted to elect him as their President.** That needs to be respected. The same holds for Biden too. If people elect him again, that needs to be respected.

People should hold media responsible when they are biased and show fake news. But a common man doesn't have the time or power or money to change it. These media outlets are owned by multibillion corporations. They can do whatever they want without much consequence.

So, it's up to us to decide how accurate is the information we are getting and **be careful not to be swayed too much on to one side or the other, based on the news you are watching. Be moderate in your approach.**

3. Maintain strict media ration: Select a few media outlets that are least biased, whether it is TV, Radio, and/or Magazines, and limit the amount of time you spend on them to less than 30 min a day. Do not participate in any negative social media campaigns/posts.

"No matter for how long you watch TV these days, its's the same topic. Trump, Trump, Trump. It's because he is the Trump card for news channels to get more viewership and thus make more money. You need to be mindful of that. I see some people being stuck to the TV almost all day, one show after another. What's **Anderson Cooper's** perspective, what's **Sean**

Hannity's opinion, what's new with **Rachel Maddow's** show, and more... **All these anchors are so good in what they do that you get pulled into their shows like a magnet.** That's the reason they are getting paid millions of dollars, and they are doing a fantastic job. But if you want to survive the election stress, you got to do a fantastic job staying away from watching too much TV" chuckled grandpa.

"But, if I stay away from watching TV and reading news, how would I stay informed about what's going on?"

"The essence of what's happening in the nation can be grasped quickly without spending hours and hours watching TV. It's the same new every day. Each day there are so many details and so many show hosts with so many perspectives. As an average person you don't need all that. Anyway, **at the end of the day it's still just a perspective of the news channel you are watching.** If you are watching FOX you get a group of experts showing why Trump is right and Biden is terrible. And if you watch CNN and MSNBC, you get a different set of people selling us why Trump is wrong all the time and Biden is great. You get the point...anyway what all you are getting is a perspective, not the Truth. Then why get bogged down in their perspective. Develop your own perspective.

That's what I did 8 years ago. The media sensationalism, I thought would end after the November 2016 elections are over. But **week after week, month after month I found them to be very ingenuous in carrying forward the sensationalism.** I realized that it never ends and it's not good for my mental health. As long as I had cable, every evening when I come home, I would just crash in the couch, turn on the TV, and would get drawn into the sensational news they have for that day. Two or three hours would lapse before I notice. These media people are so good that I couldn't restrain myself. So, **I cut the cable. Now, I am much more peaceful. My brain is not overloaded with information anymore. I control the information I let inside my brain.** Now, I gather news from different sources that are reliable and less biased. It's hard to find them though.

Some of my friends were able to maintain a strict media ration. That's another way to do it. They would spend no more than 20-30 min each day whether watching TV or listening to radio or reading news, when it pertains to politics. If you could develop strict discipline like that, that will be very helpful."

"What about social media?" asks Johnny.

"Social media is even more dangerous in my opinion. The information there is not necessarily vetted. Any one can say anything. Negative news can spread on social media like a wildfire. Things happening 10,000 miles away can ignite a firestorm of negativity here. I have seen people reacting to trivia that are not even relevant to them. Not that there are good things about social media, but negativity is easier to spread than positivity. People like to commiserate. I strongly recommend participating only in positive and meaningful discussions on social media. Stay away from negative campaigns by all means."

"That may be difficult grandpa."

"Of course, it's going to be initially. But that which is difficult becomes easy with practice" smiled grandpa. "You keep trying and keep doing it, and one day it becomes easy. And remember to Prioritize Peace of Mind. If you keep that as a top priority, it will become easy for you not to get carried away."

"I like that. I will do that" thanks for all the teaching grandpa. It's quite helpful. Just 2 days ago, before I came over here for the weekend, I was pretty depressed. My dearest friend has attempted a suicide, I was feeling hopeless too and would spend too much time on social media expressing my unhappiness, and I used to think our lives are doomed. But this weekend has made such a huge difference in my life; it's probably the best weekend I had in the past many years. I feel elated. I feel liberated from the shackles of negativity. I feel in control of my destiny. I feel good overall that my future is not decided by the President but by my own actions. I am ready to move forward. Now I feel like I know what to do with my life. Thanks so much!"

"Johnny, I am glad that we got some time to spend together this weekend. For people like me, there is no better feeling than to be of some help to younger generations."

With that, Johnny finally feels totally ready and prepared to face the election cycle but there is one last thing that's bothering him. It's his parents. Now the weekend is almost over, he will be heading back home and will have to deal with the daily bickering about politics at home. It makes it hard to remain calm in the midst of all that chaos. So, Johnny asks if Grandpa could help his parents. Grandpa says, "Long gone are the days when I could simply advice my son (your dad) and he would listen. We need to figure out a smarter way to get to him. Let me think and will get back to you."

The next day morning as Johnny is getting ready to go back home, grandpa approaches him excitingly... I got an idea!! "Isn't your birthday coming up next week? I have an amazing idea that not only helps your parents but also most of your friends and their families. Would you do it? They wouldn't refuse what you ask of them for your birthday." Without even hesitating for a second, Johnny immediately says yes!"

Grandpa explains his schema to Johnny, to invite his friends and their families for his birthday party and make sure all of them attend. He will invite Dr. Calm to attend the party as well, if he is available. It will be a nice get together and at some point of time the election topic is going to come up and he will ask Dr. Calm to have a casual conversation about this topic. I am sure most people will be curious to hear what he got to say. I know it's atypical to discuss politics in a birthday party but hey it's your birthday and you do what you like. Johnny replies, "I will do that, especially after seeing what happened to Billy because of the suicide attempt. I am sure everyone will benefit from it."

Chapter 8
Dr. Calm and the Demo-Blicans – The Party Starts

Johnny and grandpa invite Dr. Calm to give a short talk on election stress. Dr. Calm obliges.

Everyone gathers for Johnny's birthday party. After a little while, when everyone has grouped around the dinner table, Johnny takes the opportunity to ask Dr. Calm a question, innocently. "I am so concerned for myself, my family, and friends about what's going on in this nation. I mean the upcoming elections. Everyone is going crazy. Not sure what to do. Every day I must put up with some kind of negative news cycle. Family members are fighting over Trump and friendships are falling apart. In fact, it's so bad that last year one of my friend's grandmother shunned her granddaughter from Christmas party because she supported Trump. Families are falling apart. How could we put an end to this insanity, and everyone be happy again?"

Knowing the schema from Johnny's grandpa the night before, Dr. Calm understands the purpose of the question. He asks everyone around there if it is okay to answer the question, considering that politics are not welcome in most homes around the dinner table. After getting the consent from everyone there, Dr. Calm answers, I will keep it short and crisp because I don't want to spoil this nice gathering with political discussions.

"Let's go back to the time when we achieved freedom for this country in 1776. Our forefathers fought for all of us, risking their lives and got us this freedom. We did well for a while, but it saddens me that we as a nation are throwing away our freedom for nothing. We the people of this nation are not using our freedom wisely. It almost seems like we have lost our purpose as a nation. We sound more like, 'The Divided States of America' than the United States.

Here are my two cents on this topic:

1. Let's work on bringing together the divided nation, instead of cringing and cursing.
 a. Take your destiny into your hands.
 b. You can be happy no matter who your president is. Life is all about balance and the choices we make. You can be happy now!
 c. There is corruption in politics all along in the history. Sometimes it's more and sometimes it's less.
 d. As long as human ego rules the world, there will be corruption, crime, and chaos, because of greed, insecurity, and fear of the future, forgetting that the only moment that is present is NOW!
 e. People often think that getting a new President is going to drastically change their lives and propel themselves into a Utopian future. But this belief is far from the truth. A wise man knows that this world is far from perfect. In fact, very much imperfect.
 f. True happiness lies within and can be found when we learn to adjust to our circumstances, adapt to the changes in life, and move forward with courage no matter what! And this true happiness is possible because of unique human endowments we all are born with...Innate Health and Resiliency. When you tap into them, you will be happy without conditions.
 g. Be happy no matter what! Even the worst term of presidency stays only for a maximum of 8 years. Our

nation is not about just what happened in 8 years but what was built over the past 250 years.

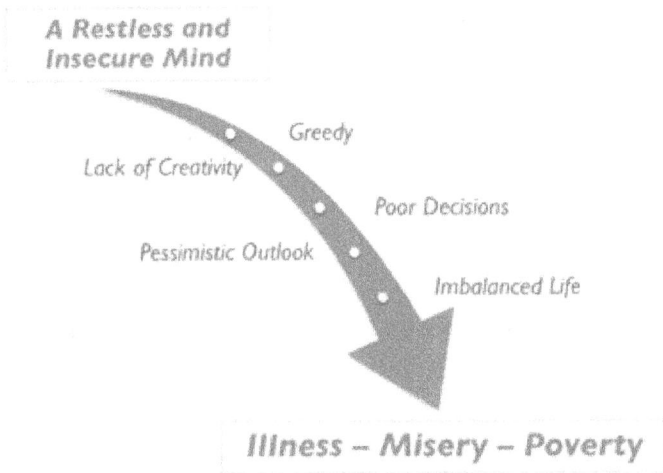

A Restless and
Insecure Mind

Greedy

Lack of Creativity

Poor Decisions

Pessimistic Outlook

Imbalanced Life

Illness – Misery – Poverty

2. I want to be a Demo-Blican, a combination of a Democrat and a Republican.

a. I don't want to be an extremist. I will use my common sense to do things that bring good to me and people around me.

b. I will not just hold on to my perspectives but will be ready to open my mind to others' perspectives and alternate possibilities.

c. I will stop criticizing. I will stop judging. I will be kind. I will be compassionate and understanding towards others.

d. My President doesn't have to do it. I am not looking for an example. I will set an example!

e. Let's elevate our collective wellbeing by being kind, loving, and compassionate human beings, spreading peace and happiness instead of contributing to the unrest and atrocities of this world.

If you like my advice, follow it. If not, it is okay to ignore it. I am always open for constructive discussion" finishes Dr. Calm with a smile.

Many guests nod their head in approval and are happy to see that someone is thinking about bringing together the divided nation.

A nice constructive discussion ensues after the dinner. One of the guests asks, "So, what do you think is going to happen to our nation? Do you think it's heading in the right direction?"

"Well, it depends on the way we look at it. **Half of the nation thinks this is a terrible time and the other half believes we are heading in the right direction.** I tend to be an optimist. I believe that everything will be alright no matter what. **There is enough good in this world that we will overcome any bad stuff happening.**

I believe everything happens for a reason. I understand that so many people are upset with what's going on with our nation, the impeachment proceedings, the constant fight between Democrats and Republicans, but **there is a Universal Plan for everything.** Many of my life experiences taught me that **even the worst possible situations in life happen for a reason.** We may not see it then but with time it will be evident. **Any difficult situation we face in life is given to us so that we may learn something from it and in the process of overcoming it, we strengthen ourselves.** If you are upset with the current political climate, don't let it destroy your peace. **Don't internalize anger and hatred.** What I know is, there is no point in holding resentment. **Anger and resentment are like hot acid that damage the person holding them more than the person it's directed towards.** We need to move on. **We need to go with flow, whatever it is. When we do that, our lives become easier.**

Also, realize that we live in a world of duality. **Good and bad, positive and negative, warm and cold, pain and pleasure, highs and lows, all these are part of the dual nature of this world.** As long as this world exists, there will be duality. In fact, without duality this world cannot exist. There will always to be ups and downs in life. **Life is a roller-coaster ride. As soon as we think we are going up, there is a downturn waiting for us.** People are excited when things are going well for them but are not ready to accept things when they are going bad. **We need to realize that whether it is good or bad, as we label them, it is just not because of us. We play a role in it but there are many factors that contribute to the outcomes we reap.**

For example, if you throw a stone from point A to point B and if there no interference, you have a fair chance that it will go in a straight line and reach the target. But if there is wind, rain, or someone else intercepting it on the way, those factors determine if the stone is going to reach the target or not. The same way, most things in life just do not depend on your skill or desire alone. **Whether for your success or failure, many factors play a role. When we realize it, we will learn to be humble.** When we do that, we won't be too excited or too depressed when things happen in life. You continue to do your best, given any situation. That's what you can really do isn't it?" pauses Dr. Calm.

"So, are you saying that Trump is not responsible for everything he is saying he has done?" asks one of the guests.

"Well, Trump took credit for all the good things that happened in his past term. But whatever good that happened was a result of many people's diligent work. Some of those things may be even because of what previous administrations have already done or laid the foundation upon which Trump had built further. To be honest and openly declare that would be a political suicide. It will put him and Republican party at risk of losing power, as Democrats will grab that opportunity and make it sound like Trump never did anything good. The opposite is also true. Democrats are afraid to admit that Republicans have done some good. They are afraid that Republicans will take advantage of their statement and propagate it during elections to stay in power.

You see there is so much fear and insecurity about losing power. The truth is no administration is 100% good or 100% bad. It's a mix of both. **No man is perfect and so none of our actions are perfect and so the results from all our actions will be less than perfect.** All of us have our own eccentricities and idiosyncrasies. In Trump's case it's publicly evident as he doesn't prefer to keep it quiet. In many politicians' cases, they keep it quiet, and we don't know what their true character is. Maybe it is better that way or maybe it is not. It's a matter of preference and our own perception.

Part of the problem is media. They constantly want to talk about Trump, whether good or bad because there is lot of talking material in there and it's entertaining. Thus, they make more money for news channels. **If the media ignores Trump completely and decides not to talk about him at all, I don't know what will happen to Trump, whether he will happy or will go crazy, but it will definitely help most of us to regain our sanity.** Media could talk about so many other good things, instead of constantly focusing on negativity. But it is not totally their fault either because **people want**

excitement and entertainment even when it's negative and harmful. Or else they feel bored and shut down the TV. That's the nature of humans.

So, ultimately you see, it's no one's fault. Everything is intertwined together, and everything is happening the way it's supposed to happen. When you realize that, you will remain peaceful. You will become even-minded. When CNN blames trump, you will not be drawn too much into it. When Fox news praises him, you will not be too excited either. You know it's a drama and the news channels have to do their part to cater to their audiences' needs.

We created all of this, collectively as human beings. **Every thought and action of ours, however small or big, will influence everyone around us directly or indirectly.** When the sum total of our thoughts and actions, collectively as human beings is more good than bad, the world progresses. When the sum total is more bad than good, the world regresses. So, I say that **if each of us take responsibility for our own thoughts and actions, and be as good as we can, that in itself is a great catalyst for positive change both nationally and globally.**

One step at a time, one person at a time, one change at a time, we will build a better world. That's what we need as a nation, whether Republican or Democrat. When we respect each other, when we are honest with each other, when we treat thy neighbor as you treat thyself, when you replace greed with self-less acts, when you find a way to be happy and content with what you have, when you extend your love and affection beyond yours family and help others, that is when we will build a bright future for all of us, overcoming the divisiveness and coming together united. Such change is what we need as a nation whether under Republican or Democrat rule. When both parties work together, finding common ground, that's when we will truly prosper."

Everyone listening to Dr. Calm intently. After a moment of silence,

"That's awesome!" exclaims one guest.

"The way to do it!" says another.

"Thumbs up! We like your ideas. We need to bring together this divided nation."

"But how do we do it?' inquire many of the guests.

"The secret is, attaining a calm mind. When people are calm and peaceful, they tend to be happy. When they are happy, they tend to be helpful and kind towards others. Also, a calm mind is a secure mind. When you feel secure, you are open to others' ideas without feeling threatened. You will be respectful of others' perspectives. When we are respectful and kind towards others, they reciprocate the same. Happy people tend to be content with what they have and so they will be less greedy.

However, **if you are constantly stressed and restless, you lead a miserable life. If you are unhappy yourself, it's hard for you to care for others. You feel insecure and feel defensive even when the other person doesn't intend bad.** Ultimately leads to conflict and your demise. When you are stressed, you tend to be reactive and less respectful of others' perspectives. When you are unhappy, you are constantly looking for happiness whether in money, possessions, relationships, sex, wine, or something else. Soon your life will be derailed unless you find true happiness. Life will be out of balance. Greed takes over.

So, my suggestion is, let's keep stress at bay. Let's learn to be calm and it will bring good. It will bring us happiness. Let's help each other be calm and happy! **Whether you are a Democrat or a Republican, let's understand each other better. Let's respect each other. Let's find common ground. Fools argue, wiseman discuss, said a great man.** Let's follow that advice. Let's be Demo-Blicans, rather than be polarized to one extreme." concludes Dr. Calm.

Dr Calm reveals a few more points on handling election stress gracefully. Everyone leaves the birthday party happily, finding a new way to think about themselves and their political affiliations – be a Demo-Blican.

Inspired by the brief talk at the party, Johnny's parents decide to see Dr. Calm in his office, hoping to resurrect their lost marriage, mainly because of political differences. The schema of Johnny and grandpa worked excellent!

Chapter 9
Resolving Political Differences and Establishing Harmony

Dr. Calm helps the couple salvage their politically conflicted marriage.

The next day, Johnny's parents meet Dr. Calm at his office. Over the past four years they have seen therapists, psychologists, and even tried medications from a psychiatrist, but couldn't really resolve their anxieties and the differences in their marriage. Both are curious how Dr. Calm could help.

Dr. Calm walks in, wearing a light blue jacket and checkered shirt on dark blue jeans. Everyone is seated comfortably. Before they could say anything, Dr. Calm says, "It's okay. No worries. I know you are wondering how I could help you. Things will unfold as we talk. I assure you that things will work out."

Johnny's parents explain that they were a good couple and had been doing fine until eight years ago when Trump came down the escalators in the Trump Tower announcing his candidacy for the 2016 Presidential election. From that day on, our marriage started falling apart. It went downhill steadily over the past 8 years.

Dr. Calm asks curiously, "That's interesting. How did that happen?" The couple explains the political differences they have, the explosive news about Trump's deeds, the 'Locker Room Talk', the current environmental policies, Trump conviction, and many other things that happened in the past 8 years, that slowly but steadily destroyed the marriage.

Dr. Calm says, "Still I don't understand. What does Trump have to do with your marriage? Do any one of you work in the White House? Do you run a news channel? I understand if Kellyanne and George Conway fought over Trump because Kellyanne worked for Trump and it's her job to support and defend Trump while George apparently was in odds with Trump. They lived near Washington D.C and I see their personal lives closely intertwined with politics. I see a lot of fuel for fire there. In their own words,

"If there's an issue, it's because she's in that job for that man, Donald Trump," George told the Washington Post.

Kellyanne suggested to the Post *that she feels torn between the two of them. "I feel there's a part of him that thinks I chose Donald Trump over him. Which is ridiculous. One is my work, and one is my marriage."*

"I feel bad for them. They both seem to be nice people. However, I don't see why you should be fighting at home constantly though. Can you please explain more? Do you have any direct information about Trump, that is not filtered at all by media? Then how do you know exactly what's going on? And even if you know, what's the point of fighting at home over something you have no control over? Don't you think your conflict at home can adversely affect your son's mental state and so his future? Please think about it."

The couple normally would have felt defensive about these questions, but Dr. Calm has a way of make them feel relaxed and receptive to his counsel. They both agreed that it's important to not fight over Trump. There are better things they could focus on to build a bright future for themselves and their son.

They express, "We are just not sure how to get over the bitter feelings and resolve the conflict within and between each other." Dr. Calm beams at them, gets up quickly, and congratulates them by holding their hands for their decision to work together to resolve their differences. "Great decision. Great decision! Don't worry about how to solve the problem. That's what I am here for. All I need is your willingness to play along. The rest will follow naturally." Let's take a few minutes break. Go have a coffee or a snack and let's be back in 10 minutes and we will discuss how to resolve conflicts and bring back harmony in our relationships. He goes on to explain the following:

    1. Absolute realities vs separate realities
    2. Conflict resolution: Seeing each other's perspective
    3. Breaking out of the prison bars of our own thoughts
    4. How to overcome bitter feelings and be kind to each other

5. The mantra for good relationships

"You mentioned earlier that you are not sure how to get over the bitter feelings and resolve the conflict within and between each other. Let's start with the conflict within first. Tell me more about why you feel conflicted."

The wife acknowledges, "I feel conflicted within because on one side, I have been a lifelong Republican and truly believe that the Republican party is the only one that can help our nation to succeed and on the other side, I disagree with some of the things Trump does."

Dr. Calm says, "I see no problem with that. You are entitled to your opinion."

The wife continues, "Since Donald Trump became our President, I started to feel conflicted within. I voted for him in the November 2016 elections and I believe that he has delivered a lot of promises he made on the campaign trail, but I don't agree with his comments on women, the way he Tweets and treats people, firing of the people who disagree with him, and more. I mean he is just not Presidential.

When I was growing up, The President of the United States has always been represented as someone who is dignified, measured, noble, kind, forgiving...an embodiment of top-notch character. I don't see any of those qualities in him. After seeing Trump, none of the kids now want to dream to become the President of the United States anymore. Yet, he is getting things done...there are many things he did that are wonderful for the country.

"So, you feel conflicted between your perception of Trump the person and Trump the President. Am I right?"

"Exactly!" exclaims the wife.

"So, on one side you feel that Mr. Donald Trump as the President of the United States, has successfully led the nation in the right direction on many fronts, what you would want as a Republican. But on the other side, you disapprove of his impulsive and abrasive behavior. Right?"

"You got it! That's the conflict I feel within. What should I do about it?"

"Well, you got to decide which one is more important for you. Can you live with Trump the personality as long as he delivers as the President?"

"That's a tough choice. I don't know."

"Okay. Let me ask you a question. Do you know Trump personally?"

"No."

"Okay. Do you know anything about the Snape character in the Harry Potter series?"

"Of course, I do. I am a big Harry Potter fan. I have read all the seven volumes, many time."

"That's great. Do you remember, starting from book one Snape is portrayed as a bad guy but in the end, he's found indeed to be a good man, helping Harry Potter, risking his life pretending to be Lord Voldemort's servant but carrying it out on Dumbledore's orders. Of course, you may not agree with Snape's personality but in the end, he delivered what he has to for Harry's survival. And Harry, when he realizes that, he cries for Snape, though he loathed him from day one he met him."

"Yes! Snape is definitely one of the most intriguing characters," replies the wife.

"So, why don't you think of Trump as Snape. May be in the end we will realize that he is not as bad as we all are being led to believe.

So, give the benefit of doubt to Trump, the person. Don't let the media coverage and the social media impressions determine who he is. You really don't know what his troubles are in the current political climate. The constant leakage of information by the insiders trying to derail him, the non-stop negative coverage by media showing him in bad light regardless of what he does, the Democrats trying to convict him from day one of Biden's taking of the Oval Office, and many others around him waiting to see his downfall! I mean that's a lot for anyone to take. Maybe he is getting more and more defensive because of all the incoming negativity that he must deal with. Don't get me wrong, I am not defending his personality. I am just trying to put things in perspective. Of course, I also believe that most of it is Mr. Trump's own making whether intentional or unintentional.

So, if you think he is carrying out the duties well as the President, do not be bothered too much by his personality. It is what it is. He is 78 years old now. **If he didn't change all this time, I doubt he will change now. Accepting him for what he is, will make your life easier.**

I always give benefit of doubt to people who I do not personally know, no matter what other people say about them. *We truly do not know other people in our life, especially when we haven't had a direct interaction with them and haven't spent hours and hours trying to sincerely understand who they are. What all we have is our perception of them. This is further mired by others' perception of them. This is true even in the closest of our relationships, like* *marriage. We think we know them, but we truly don't.* **The reason why most marriages fall apart is because either one or both never made the effort to truly understand the other...all they have is their perception of the other but not who truly they are.** *Where there is no understanding, there will be no love. Where there is no love, there will be only pretense but no true caring. Slowly conflict creeps in and ultimately the relationship falls apart."*

The wife and husband, both are listening to Dr. Calm carefully. They exchanged a quickly look, trying to assess whether they truly understand each other or not.

"So, are you saying that what all I have is perception of Trump based on what other people are saying but I truly do not know him. Then my decisions should be guided by whether I support his policies or not rather than his personality? If that is the case, my answer is clear. I do believe the country was going in the right direction in his Presidency. We were strong and doing well, no matter what others think of us. Thank you so much. This has cleared my head about Mr. Trump and has resolved the conflict in my heart about who should I vote for this upcoming election season."

The husband has been quietly and patiently listening to all this conversation for almost half an hour and he couldn't hold back anymore. "That doesn't make any sense. I am sorry. I disagree Dr. Calm. Trump did so many bad things. He just can't be forgiven for the things he did to our nation and its people," says with his ears fuming with anger.

Dr. Calm calmly replies "Yes, my friend. Please continue. I do see that you disagree. Can you please tell me what do you disagree with? I am curious to know more."

The husband cools down a little bit, seeing that Dr. Calm is not offended by his outburst and is ready to listen to his side of the story. He continues, "My wife is a wonderful person. I don't disagree with that. But, supporting Trump...I can't agree with that."

"Why?" asks Dr. Calm.

"I don't think he is appropriate to be our President. He doesn't represent our values as a nation and its people. He has done so many bad things."

"Like?" calmly inquires Dr. Calm.

"Look, he sets a bad example for us and our kids. I can't let my kids watch him or read about him. I am just worried they are going to learn bad things from him. That's not the way to behave. That's not the way to Tweet. You don't disparage people around you. You don't throw tantrums for every little thing. I mean, look at our allies and other countries. They are sneering at us because of his behavior. Trump has made all of us Americans a laughingstock in front of the world. He doesn't get along with any of the world leaders. He thinks he gets along, but they all laugh at him, behind his back. He even had a row with the Pope. I mean, that's really crazy."

"I do see there are things about Mr. Trump that you absolutely detest," responds Dr. Calm.

"I do and I am openly vocal about it," replies the husband.

"And I do believe that you have the right to your opinion," replies Dr. Calm.

"Yes, I do, and I think I am right."

"I don't see anything wrong about you having your opinion or thinking that you are right," says Dr. Calm.

"Thank you, Dr. Calm."

"I don't see any problem to solve here though" says Dr. Calm.

The husband confusedly looks at him and says, "Well, this opinion of mine and disagreement with my wife is causing us trouble. We are in constant conflict. How do we resolve it?"

Dr. Calm smiles pleasantly, "The first thing is to understand that we live in separate realities. I respect the reality you live in."

"Hmm. Can you tell me more?" inquires the husband.

"Sure.

Each of us live in our own personal reality. Our personal reality is determined by the environment we in which we were brought up, the experiences we had in life, our upbringing, the place we were born in, your personality, your education, your field of work, and many other things. Ultimately, based on all that, you think differently about a given situation.

A person born in a Democrat family and brought up in California, a blue state, his reality will be different than someone who is born and brought up by a Republican family in Texas, a red state.

For example, let's say Donald Trump said, "We are getting along well with Russian President Vladimir Putin. That's great! Absolutely great!"

"As you know, a Democrat's view of this statement by Trump will be totally different from that of a Republican's. While the Republican may say that it's a good thing to get along with powerful nations like Russia so that we reduce the risk of conflict with them whether in the form of Cold War or a real war, a Democrat will immediately denounce the Republican view, saying that Trump is naïve or maybe he is colluding with Russia.

After spending millions of dollars investigating the issue of collusion with Russia by Mueller probe, we the people still do not know the entire truth, the actual reality of the situation. Democrats maintain that Trump is still guilty while Republicans refute it.

The point here is, **depending on your perspective, the reality you see changes. In any given situation, there is one absolute reality and multiple relative realities.**

We live in a world of separate realities, but we often forget that. Deeply stuck in our own perspectives, we think that our reality is the only one existent. That's the basis for all conflict whether political or personal.

When people start acknowledging that the other person has equal right to their own perspective, how much ever crazy it may sound for us and be respectful of their reality, there will be less conflict in this world.

You see, your wife has her right to hold on to her reality, even though you think it's totally crazy. And you mentioned that she is a wonderful woman, and you love her. Then let us not confuse who she is as a person with what she believes politically.

Does it make sense?" pauses Dr. Calm.

The husband listening carefully replies "Yes. She is a wonderful woman. I see that the person who she is, has nothing to do with her political affiliations. Based on her upbringing and her lifelong exposure to Conservative philosophy, her political reality is shaped. I see that. I see that clearly now. How come I didn't see that until now? I should have known. Her parents, her friends, and the place where she grew up in are strong Republican foot holds. It's only natural to be a Republican for her. She learnt whatever she learnt, not because she wants to but because that is what she was exposed to from early childhood. And I know that our environment plays a huge role in shaping who we are. **Oh my God! That's a huge revelation to me.** It's just dawned upon me that she didn't have almost any other choice. I am sure she must be conflicted so much within, trying to deal with me and yet holding on to what she learnt all her life while being conflicted about Trump. I am so sorry for being judgmental. I am really sorry" says the husband with tear filled eyes.

The wife sitting next to him feels totally emotional, "It's alright. You didn't know you were stuck in your own perspective. You are a good man just trying to convince me of what you think was right and good for the nation.

I know you don't get any checks from Biden for convincing me to go against Trump," smiles the wife.

Both, feeling emotional, exchange looks with tear filled eyes, holding each other's hands. Seems the emotional gap between them is closing down. There is a moment of silence.

Dr. Calm excuses himself, "I am getting an urgent phone call. Do you mind if I step out for a couple of minutes?"

The wife and husband, sitting there, take a few minutes to settle down. They whisper in each other's ears "I am glad that we came in here. Let's see what else he has for us to learn."

Dr. Calm returns in a couple of minutes, "So, how are you guys doing?"

"Doing good," smilingly replies the couple. "I don't know what kind of magic this is. We saw many therapists and counselors. They used to make us talk about all the bad things that happened in the past so that they could understand us better and help us let go of the bad emotions. But each time, we would come home feeling worse. And here we are seeing you for the first time and we feel like the problem we have is almost solved. We don't understand it," puzzlingly inquires the couple.

Dr. Calm breaks out in laughter. "I am sure the therapists and counselors were doing their best to help you. They have a certain way to do things and my ways are a little different. It just turned out that this way worked for you better.

I don't believe in digging into people's past because every time we dig into the bad memories of the past, we resurface the bad feelings associated with them. Whatever happened in your past, whether it is yesterday or four years ago, it's just a memory in your mind. It doesn't exist anymore unless you decide to bring it back to life, thinking about it.

Each time you dig out traumatic memories, you potentiate the bad feelings associated with them. Of course, there are times we need to let people explain their situations so that we can understand them; but beyond that I don't like to dwell on the past unless they are good memories," smilingly replies Dr. Calm.

"Well, whatever you did, we feel good. Is there anything else we need to know?"

"One more thing I would like to mention is, you remarked earlier that you think you are right about your perspective about Trump, and you are vocal about it. What I would say is, **you absolutely have the right to believe** that you are right! But we should not impose on others what we think is right, especially when we know that they hold a different position on that topic. If we insist that ours is the only right perspective, we are asking for conflict. Does it make sense?"

"Yes, it makes sense. Sometimes we both forget that we are stuck in our own perspectives, and we impose our ideas on each other. We will try to scale that back. We also realize, most things are simply a matter of perspective and we all live in separate realities. Both of us can be right in our own ways though we may not agree with each other, and we can be respectful of the world the other person is living in," replies the couple.

"Exactly. And if you ever forget this and get into trouble mode, remember this **Mantra for good relationships: avoid false assumptions, clarify when needed, and always try to understand.** Most relationships fall apart because of false assumptions. These false assumptions often start trivial and slowly grow to giant differences in opinions, resulting in major conflicts. If you follow this, you will never fail your relationships. You can't clap with one hand and so, just one spouse alone can't salvage a stressed relationship.

Both of you must practice this mantra and it will save you from much suffering. Hope you both have a nice day," concludes Dr. Calm.

Both the wife and husband feel good to have their differences resolved. But they know that once they go home the constant barrage of negative news and discussions with friends and family about the elections is going to pull them down. So, they asked if they could do anything to 'stay happy and peaceful no matter what's going on around them'. Dr. Calm says, "Of course yes, if you are willing to take the necessary steps for reclaiming the lost happiness and balance in your lives, I am going to share with you what less than 1% population knows about **FINDING TRUE HAPPINESS.** I will see you next week."

Chapter 10
Reclaiming Your Lost Happiness

**The happy couple understands the true source
of happiness in their lives.**

A week later, Johnny's parents return to Dr. Calm' office.

"So, how are things going?" inquires Dr. Calm.

Both the wife and husband say at once, "Amazing! We feel so much better. The hard feelings have been dissolved. We appreciate each other for who we are, and we are keeping aside our political differences. We understand that we may not agree on everything, but we can still respect each other's perspectives."

"That's great!"

"But every time we turn on TV, read something on social media, or hear a comment about the upcoming elections, we find it hard to restrain ourselves from discussing politics. Often that leads to some turmoil within. Especially, my husband feels unhappy seeing or hearing about Trump and starts saying something which I don't like. How do we solve this problem?" asks the wife.

"I see. What makes you so unhappy when you think of Trump?" asks Dr. Calm.

The husband quickly replies, "Everything about him. Starting with his hair, the orange tan, the long red tie, the things he says on TV, his policies, and his comments on women...there's a lot that I don't like about him. He makes me feel upset and unhappy."

"Hmm, that's a lot for sure!" chuckles Dr. Calm. "Would you like to work on it and be happy no matter who your President is and what your opinion of him is?"

"Of course. That will save me lots of stress. Moreover, I am afraid he may be reelected, and I will have to bear with him as our President for another four years."

"Alright!!" enthusiastically says Dr. Calm. "I am going to share with you something powerful that helps to build a lasting foundation of peace and joy in your life; actually, very few people know about it. And we will take it from there. You ready?

"Yes, we are ready!" the couple reciprocate Dr. Calm's enthusiasm.

"Okay. Let me introduce to you to 'Innate Health and Resilience', two powerful gifts we were endowed with by birth.

Let me ask you a question, what is the most important thing for a human being?

The couple thinks for a minute, exchanging looks at each other but do not say anything.

Dr. Calm continues, "**The greatest necessity for any human being is to be happy, peaceful, and secure. The highest goal for all of us is to rise above suffering whether it is physical, mental, or spiritual.** None of us want suffering, right? We all want to be peaceful, secure, and happy. Isn't it?

"Right" both nod their head simultaneously.

"Then what is preventing us to be so?" asks Dr. Calm.

As the wife and husband look at him for the answer, he continues, "Our wrong concept of happiness and not knowing of how to find true happiness. Our forgetfulness of who we truly are and falling down from our natural state of wellbeing."

The couple continues to listen, inquisitively.

Dr. Calm continues, "Let's discuss Innate Health and Resiliency. That will help you understand my statement above.

Innate Health is your natural state of mental wellbeing where your happiness is unconditional; that means your happiness is not dependent on any external conditions. We all are born that way, peaceful and joyful.

If you carefully observe, as little babies we were happy as long as our physiologic needs were met. As little kids, we were happy for no reason. We didn't bother if we were black or white, we didn't know how much money our parents had in their bank accounts, we didn't care which country you belong to...we were just naturally happy. It's because we didn't have any external conditions to be met to be happy. We played and we had fun.

However, as we grew our happiness got conditioned to certain things. As a toddler, it's a toy. As a teenager it's a bike. As a young adult, may be your first love or the first car. Then it's a dream house or a dream job or something else. Slowly, we started falling away from our natural state of mental wellbeing, our Innate Health, a state of unconditional happiness to a state of conditional happiness, where our happiness became dependent on external circumstances. This **dependence on external circumstances for our happiness is the root cause of our suffering.** Remember, once you were happy without any conditions. You were truly peaceful and joyful.

This truth will be quickly evident when you see the little kids playing. They have a knack of putting themselves in a happy state of mind, no matter what. I call it a natural state for us because those kids do not have to read anything about happiness, they don't have to meditate, they don't have to attend a seminar..." smilingly continues Dr. Calm "they are just naturally happy! That's how we all were born at some point of time in our life. Then what happened? Because of our environment, our parental upbringing, what we learn at school, what we watch on TV, from our society, and these days the social media, we learn to be happy if certain conditions are met.

If I have this then I will be happy, *if* I achieve this goal then I will be happy, *if* I feel approved by my parent I will be happy, *if* I am loved by this girl I will be happy, *if* I get that job I will be happy, *if* Trump is defeated I will be happy, *if* Trump wins I will be happy...and the more number of 'ifs' you have, the harder it will be for you to be happy. **Unfortunately, our society pushes us to add more and more 'ifs' to our list**...the American Dream, isn't it? The problem is, **the more 'ifs' you have the harder for you to be happy** because your happiness is dependent on achieving something or getting what you want. **This is where the American Dream fails big.** It doesn't account for the fact that all those achievements, money, popularity, and possessions may or may not bring you any happiness. In fact, in the process of achieving them you may lose your happiness.

It's simply a false mental construct that we were made to believe by the media, Hollywood, and the society around us that accomplishing things and having more equals happiness. It's the **wrong concept of happiness** that we were taught from early childhood. I mean, it's just not America, the whole world is conditioned to believe it. But research shows that after you make certain amount of money, to live comfortably and take care of your loved ones, more money doesn't not make you happy anymore. In fact, it may have an inversely proportional relationship to your happiness. That is where we all falter as a society. This wrong concept of happiness is killing us, being stressed out every day, chasing the endless dreams, working harder and harder for less and less return, leaving our inner happiness behind. You see, **the whole society was built on the wrong concept of happiness.**

When was the last time you heard the wise old adages like 'be happy with what you have, a content man is more fortunate than a wealthy man, health is wealth, do not seek more than what you need?' The modern society has led us astray from what's truly valuable and that which really matters to lead a happy life. We think we are advanced technologically, but we are losing ourselves in technology and the advances of the modern society.

Don't get me wrong. It's important to advance technologically, it's important to set and achieve goals, and it's important to make money, but do not think that's what gives you happiness. **Do not mistake your goals, achievements, and possessions for happiness. That's the biggest mistake we make as a society.** The media portrays shiny cars, big homes, muscular body, beautiful figure, being rich and popular etc. as a standard for success and happiness. The truth is far from that. We know many celebrities who are deeply depressed and unhappy. Some of our most favorite Hollywood Stars died of stress, depression, suicides, or drugs. It's sad isn't it? It's because they have drifted far away from their natural state of mental wellbeing, falling prey to wrong concepts of happiness and success, created by our society, falsely portrayed by the media.

I feel bad for those celebrities, millionaires, doctors, lawyers, and the so-called successful people who are totally stressed and are losing their souls in their pursuit of happiness in the wrong places. That's what we got change! To help them back to the basic understanding that we all are innately healthy. **We were born happy and peaceful. That's who we are. Peace of mind is our true nature. We don't need to add anything to us to make us happy. We may go ahead and achieve what we want if that serves a purpose but, in the process, do not lose sight of your true happiness.**

A time will come in our lives, where we will be tested by life's challenges. All that we have will be gone, whether it's money and possessions because of a financial downfall, whether it's a relationship breakdown or divorce, whether it's loss of loved ones, or something else that wipes us out completely. **During those times we may feel sad and we may feel we have lost our happiness. But the truth is what we have lost is our conditional happiness. Our unconditional happiness, our innate state of natural wellbeing is intact.**

If we don't lose sight of this truth, when life challenges us, we will be less disturbed by them. We will recover faster from them. We can look within ourselves and find our true happiness and we feel at peace. We remain unperturbed by the challenging experiences of life. You feel at ease. You learn from the experience and move on gracefully. Anyway, that's the only viable way to thrive.

You see, **if you let go of the mental constructs of how things should be and what makes you happy as defined by the society, you will free yourself from many limitations. That's where your journey towards your real happiness begins,"** concludes Dr. Calm, leaning back into the chair.

The couple, deeply absorbed in digesting Dr. Calm's words, take a moment to pause and reflect what they just heard.

"So, being happy and peaceful is our natural state that we are born with. That's our innate health and it is intact no matter what happens in life because that's who we are at our core...our true nature is peace and joy. We all have this Innate Health regardless of our age, sex, race, country, political affiliations etc. When we run into trouble if we remember our true nature that we were once happy without any conditions, it helps us get back to a happy state of mind quickly. Is that accurate?" the couple recites what they learnt.

"Perfectly summarized! And that leads us to discuss Resilience, our innate capacity to bounce back from a stressful state to a peaceful state of mind. Resilience is our innate capacity to be flexible with life, overcome challenges, and reclaim your lost peace and joy in life. It is our capacity to recover and heal.

We all slide up and down on what I call, 'The Stress-Peace Continuum.' No matter how smart and careful we are, things happen in life. Life is full of surprises. You never know what kind of trouble is waiting for you in the next corner. **Problems often come unannounced, whether it is a health issue, financial failure, political setback, a relationship breakdown or something else.** We get dragged into bad emotions and stressful situations. When that happens and when we slide down from the state of peace and joy to stress and misery, we need to get back to our normal selves as quickly as possible. Resilience is that inner capacity of yours that helps you slide back up to your peaceful self.

We all are endowed with this gift of Resilience by birth. And the more you use this gift, the more powerful it becomes. When life trials shroud you and when your emotional strength is tested, instead of giving up if you stand strong and fight, your Inner Resilience strengthens.

Life tests must be seen as opponents that are training you to get stronger, in preparation for the next challenge. For example, a boxer who always fights with a weak opponent, never gets stronger. Only by fighting a stronger opponent, he becomes stronger and one day he will win the world championship. The same way, every challenge in your life is preparing you for the next phase of your life so that you may ultimately emerge victorious in the game of life."

"That's an interesting metaphor and an amazing way to look at life challenges," says the husband approvingly.

Dr. Calm thanks him and continues, "So, when you realize that you are born peaceful and joyful, and that you always have your Innate Health intact within, no matter how much trouble you are in and how many trials you went through, and that you could access it in no time and bounce back from a stressful state to a peaceful state, using your Inner Resilience, suddenly you feel a sense of freedom. Life doesn't seem that difficult anymore. You feel you could always fall back to your natural state of mental wellbeing, no matter what's going on. And when you are there, the problems that are plaguing you lose their power over you. They dissolve and disappear like smoke that dissipates into the air. You reclaim our lost peace and joy.

And when we learn to be peaceful and joyful consistently, that's when the magic happens. Things start flowing well. You spot new opportunities. You prosper. You accomplish what you need while remaining balanced and content. It's the opposite of chasing the American Dream where you go after everything else, seeking happiness in the wrong places, ultimately reaping misery instead of true happiness."

"Hmm, are you saying that chasing the American Dream is wrong?" asks the husband.

"No actually. You can chase any dream you want whether, American, Chinese, or Indian, as long as you are aware that your true happiness lies within you and not in chasing those dreams," smilingly replies Dr. Calm.

"Well, that sounds exciting. **I could still chase my dreams, set goals, and achieve things. I just have to be careful to not equate my happiness with those goals and achievements. Otherwise, if I fail to achieve them, I will feel devastated.** That's what I see sometimes where people feel like they lost everything when in fact, they only had a minor failure on their path to success. That's because of false identification of their happiness with something external to them, I guess."

"Exactly!" responds Dr. Calm.

"Are you also saying that being stressful is not our natural state? My friends say that I am born stressful and that's who I am. Just because I am stressed often that doesn't mean that's who I am right?" asks the husband seeking reassurance.

"Not at all!" says Dr. Calm reassuringly tapping on his shoulder. "**Just because you are used to being stressed a lot that doesn't mean that you are born that way.** Things happen in life and because none of us get any kind of teaching on how to handle stress whether at school, or home, we develop maladaptive patterns and wrong coping mechanisms. Eventually, we get used to staying stressful. But always remember that peace and joy is our true nature. That's how we are born. That's the reason we can stay confident that we can go back there anytime, our home, just with a little bit of learning and proper guidance."

"Oh man! That's a big relief for me. I thought I am going to die stressed! I have some hope it seems!" laughs the husband with a sigh of relief.

"Then I am saved too!" the wife breaks out in laughter, "It seems there is cure for my husband's constant worry and anxiety about everything."

The wife continues, "All this makes so much sense, though it's quite different from what we learnt all our lives. I wonder why no one ever told us about these inner capacities and gifts we are endowed with. It's so simple and practically applicable. It seems logical, especially observing the little children at home. If their toy is broken, they may cry for a little bit, but they come right back and play with something else. **Kids have a knack of putting themselves in a happy state of mind quickly, no matter what happens, unlike we adults who brood over things for days, weeks, and months, sometimes about trivial stuff.** I believe it's because of our conditioning. It is we as parents and the society that's teaching them wrong concepts of happiness and condition their happiness. How do we reverse that conditioning? How do we stay happy consistently?" enquires the wife.

And most importantly, how do we apply this to the upcoming elections and remain peaceful during this political season?"

"That's the reason I created a simple three step system, called the 'P-E-T System for Stress-free Living'. It helps people find calm and be happy consistently. I will share that with you during our next visit.

Coming back to politics, it's like anything else in life. If you decide that you are going to be happy only if your candidate wins, your mind will follow your instruction. You will be quite unhappy if your candidate loses. But, if you determine to be happy no matter who wins, whether it is to your liking or not, you will be fine even if your candidate ends up losing. Life moves on. **Our destiny and our happiness are decided more by what happens in our house every day rather than what happens in the White House.**

I don't know who is going to win. No one can predict the future, but we can be prepared. That doesn't mean you give up political activism. **You continue to do what you got to, to help and support your candidate. Just don't get into fights with others in this process. Hope for the best, prepare for the worst.** Don't let political issues or Trump's Twitterstorms spoil your peace of mind. Do not condition your happiness to political outcomes.

Whether you are a Democrat or a Republican, it is a mental construct that you have created in your mind that you will be happy only when your candidate wins. That's habitual thinking. That's conditional happiness. Don't fall prey to it. Does it make sense?" asks Dr. Calm.

"Yes. It makes sense. Just realizing that it is a mental construct helps a lot. I see that I made it up. And I can unmake it!" says the husband.

"Exactly! You can undo any conditioning you have in your mind. Understanding this fact in itself is liberating."

With this they both feel confident that they can be happy in life no matter what. Then they ask if there are any specific tools that could help them to build upon what they learnt, to be calm and happy consistently in life.

"Absolutely! We can continue our conversation during the next visit, where I will reveal to you the secret to calmness" concludes Dr. Calm.

"Sure, we will see you soon!" exclaim the happy couple.

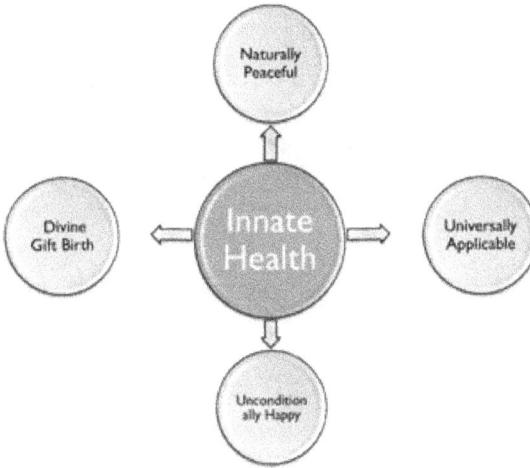

Naturally
Peaceful

Divine
Gift Birth

Innate
Health

Universally
Applicable

Uncondition
ally Happy

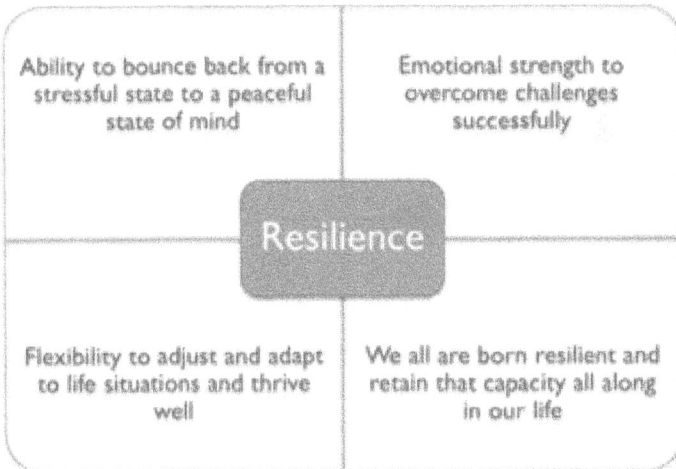

Ability to bounce back from a stressful state to a peaceful state of mind

Emotional strength to overcome challenges successfully

Resilience

Flexibility to adjust and adapt to life situations and thrive well

We all are born resilient and retain that capacity all along in our life

Knowing that We Slide Up and Down, Helps Fight Stress

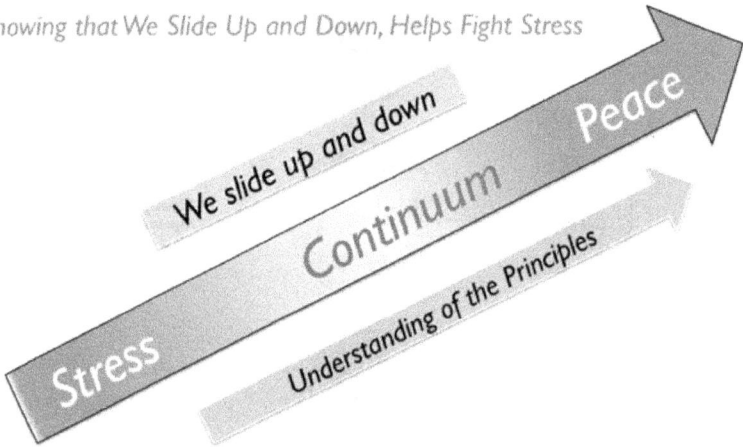

We slide up and down

Peace

Continuum

Stress

Understanding of the Principles

Chapter 11
Why Should We Be Calm?

The thief of happiness is revealed.

The couple comes back a week later. Dr. Calm inquires how things are going.

"They are going really well. We haven't argued for two weeks straight. That's a record. Past four years we are used to fighting at least twice a week if not twice a day. We are just not used to it, that's all," the couple smiles happily.

The wife continues, "Now, my husband doesn't anxiously react to every little thing. He has become much calmer since our last discussion. But every now and then he gets instigated when he watches news on TV. We are thinking, how to prevent even that little instigation. We know that it builds up and soon derail us back to a stressful state. How can we deepen our calmness and do even better? We like this feeling of calm."

"Sure. Will be happy to help. Let me share with you, the P-E-T System for Stress-Free Living. Before that, I will give you a small exercise to do. I will be back in 5 minutes and then we will discuss about it. Here is the exercise: Sit quietly. Do not talk to each other. Do not look at each other. Consider that you are alone in this room. Close your eyes. Count from 100 to 1. Do not let your mind wander while you do that. For example, if you started at 100 and counted back up to 70 and then your mind wanders and thinks about the lunch you are going to have this afternoon or what Trump said at Prayer Breakfast or something else, then you got to start counting from 100 again. Until you finish counting from 100 to 1 without your mind wandering off, you haven't completed the exercise. Makes sense?" asks Dr. Calm.

"Makes sense" reply the couple.

"Okay then. I will be back in five minutes."

Five minutes pass by and Dr. Calm opens the door and asks the couple, "Are you done?"

"Not yet, we need more time," quickly respond the couple.

"Alright. Let's take another five minutes."

Dr. Calm comes back after another five minutes, "How is it going?"

"Err...do you think we can have some more time to do the exercise?"

"Well, you have all the time in the world to practice this exercise, but I will guarantee you that you will spend the rest of the day doing it. Let's chat a little bit and we will figure out what to do next," smiles Dr. Calm. "So, tell me what happened? Who wants to go first?"

The wife replies, "This is a wicked exercise. I thought it was going to be easy and why were you asking us to do such a silly thing. Then as I started counting, the first time by the time I reached 90 from 100, I was already gone somewhere...back at my home planning what I got to do for dinner tonight. I was lost in thought for a couple of minutes and then came back to the present and realized what happened. I started over again, and this time I was able to get up to 70 when my mind drifted away to see how my husband is doing. He was sitting there with closed eyes and I was curious what's going on inside his head. And then I heard the knock on the door from you," completes the wife.

"What about you?" Dr. Calm asks the husband.

He replies, "Huh! I thought I was the only one having this problem. Glad to here that I am not the only one struggling. I started out fine, I was able to get from 100 to 75 without any difficulty and then I started thinking about a project I have to finish this week. I started calculating the number of hours I have to put into it and what would happen if I can't finish it and all of a sudden, I realized that I got to finish this exercise. I came back to start the reverse counting again but you were already knocking on the door by that time. It's insane. Time went by so fast"

"Good. Thanks for sharing. What happened the next time?"

"I was determined this time and was able to get to 51 but then I remembered the article I read this morning about 'A Blue Wave is Rising in the Cities' depicting Democrat win in major cities. I started thinking about the upcoming primaries and then I drifted off," admits the wife.

"I think I didn't do too bad the second time. I was able to count to 39 when the project came back to my mind again. I was thinking how to convince my boss to approve this project and how to make it successful. Then I started thinking about my last project a few months ago where I was scolded by my boss because I didn't finish it on time. Then I heard the knock on the door again," smiles the husband.

"It's interesting that we were not able to do a simple exercise like this without daydreaming" chuckles the husband.

"I think we both failed the test abysmally, right?" asks the worried wife.

Dr. Calm pleasantly smiles and responds, "I wouldn't look at it as a failure. I would simply see it as something to learn from.

Human mind is restless. It's preoccupied. It likes to wander, and we find it hard to stay in the present moment and concentrate. We drift off to the past or the future. Now imagine how much time we spend like that in a day...my guess is, a lot.

So what? What's the problem with being restless? You may ask.

The problem is, **restlessness is the thief of happiness. When you are restless, you can't focus.** When you can't focus, you can't perform well. When you don't perform well, things are not done on time and even if they are done, not at the highest level of quality. So, a restless mind makes you less efficient. You miss our deadlines. Your boss will be unhappy, and you will be unhappy too. You see, it's all connected.

Also, **a restless mind is foggy. When your mind is foggy, you run into all sorts of trouble.** It's like driving a car when there's fog ahead. You can't see clearly. You may get into an accident. The higher the density of fog, the lesser the clarity in moving ahead, and the greater the risk or getting into an accident. The same way, the greater the restlessness of our mind, the lesser the clarity on how to move forward with life situations. **If you notice, restless often leads to indecisiveness...the back and forth when making important decisions. In such a state of mind, we often end up making wrong choices or mistakes, which lead to unnecessary complications.** That wastes time and energy. It's a vicious cycle and that's how most people spend all their lives, never knowing why they always have bad luck and why they have to go through so much trouble, and they work hard and never get the right results. It's their restlessness that is putting obstacles on their path to success. The way to exit that vicious cycle is to find deep calmness. Makes sense?"

"Wow! We never thought restlessness has so much impact on our lives. We just thought it's normal and harmless," responds the couple.

"Well, it feels normal because we are so used to it. Everyone around us is restless too and that's the way we grew up and that's how most people are. But, once you feel deep calmness, you suddenly realize how restless you were in the past and how much more effectively you can live when you are calm. I mean, when you are calm, your mind will be clear of all restless thoughts. You see things clearly, spot opportunities easily and act on them quickly, make less mistakes, efficiently finishing tasks at hand, meeting the deadlines on time...you are happy, your boss is happy, your company or business performs better...the benefits are needless. When you are efficient, you finish work faster and you will have more time for hobbies and to spend with your family. You can live a life of balance.

So, that's the reason I say, 'Calmness First'. **When we make Calmness a priority, everything else in life falls into its place.**

When you are calm within, you automatically manufacture happiness from within. I often find that after I have a deep meditation and go to work, I notice everyone smiling at me. Soon I realize that they are smiling back at me because they're seeing a smile on my face. This happens naturally. I notice I access the happy place within me, my innate health, when I am deeply calm."

"That's amazing. We would want that" quickly respond the couple. "So, how do we access calm?"

"Well, that brings us to the P-E-T system.

I recommend you practice this system regularly. It melts away stress instantaneously and brings calmness to your lives!

Let me ask you a question? What do you do every day in the morning?"

"Well, we get up, get ready, brush our teeth, take a shower, eat breakfast, and work out a little bit."

"Good. How much time do you spend for all that? Possibly an hour or two."

"Okay. Do you eat lunch? Do you eat dinner?"

"Yes."

"How much time do you spend for that?"

"Possibly another hour or so."

"Okay. You spend almost 2-3 hours a day to feed your body and take care of it. Right?"

"Right. Anything wrong with it?" ask the couple puzzled.

"Oh! Not at all. That's good. Now, tell me, how much time you spend each day, taking care of your mind?"

They both look at each other and answer quizzically, "Almost none. Didn't know we have to."

"Hmm. You see the problem?" asks Dr. Calm.

"No, what is it?" reply the couple.

"You spend a lot of time doing everything else but not spend anytime taking care of your mind. Isn't it the reason so many of us have a problem with our minds...being stressed and restless?"

"Huh! That's interesting. Never thought about it!" says the husband.

"Let me ask you a question. What happens if you don't brush your teeth for a week?"

The husband and wife look at each other with googly eyes, "Well we don't want to imagine. We are going to stink," they both laugh out loud.

"Exactly, that's what happens to our mind also if we don't take care of it regularly. It's going to stink with overloaded information, hurt feelings from the past, worries about the future, things other people say about you, and more. You see, we get exposed to a lot in our lives every day and our brains absorb everything around. **It's our duty to unclutter our brain and empty our mind of restless thoughts.** You do it by practicing deep calmness daily. It dissolves restlessness and you find peace and joy."

The husband and wife are listening attentively.

Dr. Calm continues, "Did you ever wonder why so many people are mentally ill in this world? **America is the richest nation on the earth. Yet we have so much mental health problem in our society. Why? It's because we are not taught how to take care of our minds.** We don't know how to keep stress at bay. No one teaches us how to be calm and happy. We spend lots of time on money making, going out and partying, putting on make-up, getting the nails and hair done, shopping for nice clothes, but we don't even spend a fraction of that time on practicing calmness. No one teaches us the art and science of true happiness. That's the reason we are a stressed nation."

Dr. Calm pauses for a moment. He continues with a tear in his eye, "It bothers me that we as human beings suffer a lot because we don't give ourselves enough time to learn and practice that which really brings true happiness to us. We somehow forget that it is important. We fall for the delusion of non-stop running around for one thing after another, getting stuck in the rat race."

"Yes, that's very true," both husband and wife quietly nod their head. "If you teach us, we promise that we will spend enough time each day to practice the system and once we learn, we will teach others also."

"And that is going to guard you from election stress or some other stress," smiles Dr. Calm. "Let's take a short break and we will come back in a few minutes to discuss the 'P-E-T' system."

Chapter 12
Anchoring Yourself in Calm

The P-E-T System for Stress-Free Living.

After they come back from a short break, Dr. Calm continues, "Here is the P-E-T system. 'P' stands for Three Principles, 'E' stands for 'Two Relaxation Exercises' and 'T' stands for a Calming Technique. All these three components of the P-E-T system work together and each of the components is important in its own way to bring peace and joy to your life."

The Three Principles
The Golden Key to Stress Freedom

Dr. Calm continues, "Let's start with the Three Principles. They were originally discovered by Mr. Sydney Banks in 1973. They are Universal Principles applicable to all of us in all situations, whether elections or no elections. They help us understand the nature of our mind. As that new understanding dawns upon you, life becomes more enjoyable and less hectic. You feel at peace. That is what happened to me almost a decade ago when I was in deep distress. That new understanding hit me like a flash and all the negativity in me disappeared like magic. I was left with profound peace and joy within. I couldn't understand how that was possible because ten minutes prior I was in deep distress and my entire world was falling apart. I have been stressed out for months. Yet, just with 10 minutes of listening to the Principles, all the restless thoughts in my mind, running at million miles per second came to a sudden halt, as if someone pushed brakes on them urgently.

None of the circumstances in my life changed, yet I felt peaceful within. How was that possible? It's miraculous.

Those 'Three Principles' are Mind, Consciousness, and Thought."

Dr. Calm pauses for a moment. He continues, "Don't listen to my words. Don't look at the definitions alone. Look for the meaning behind the words. Look for the feeling behind. You got feel them. It's not about intellectual study or memorization of the definitions. You got to understand them by experiencing them.

I know, I know...you are thinking, "What does he mean by that?" You will understand this with time. Be patient. Be curious. Be open to new possibilities. Sometimes, the understanding of the Principles dawn upon you instantly and sometimes it takes time. Each person's experience is different."

Both the husband and wife nod their head in agreement.

Dr. Calm continues,

"The *Mind* is the intelligent energy behind all life. *Mind* is the power that makes *life* possible. It is the power of *Mind* that creates and sustains, everything in the universe.

Thought is the intelligent force that directs you through life and helps navigate it. It is rudder of life. It takes you where you want to go.

Consciousness is the intelligent power that gives us the ability to be aware of our experiences in life.

We are all born with these three divine gifts. Your destiny depends on how you use these gifts.

The Mind

Your mind can be compared to the engine of a car. A car does not move forward if the engine malfunctions; likewise, your life will not move forward if your mind is dysfunctional. For the car, the engine is the source of all energy and power. For your life, your mind is the source of all energy and power. You rely on the power of your mind to do well in life.

If you let Trump or the election stress bother you to the point where you become extremely restless and your mind becomes agitated, you will find it difficult to focus on important things that matter in your life. I have seen a lot of people who are so distracted by Trump's comments that they can't function properly. They are paralyzed by fear, anger, anxiety, and all the other negative emotions. Remember, the negative emotions you hold within cause more damage to you than to the other person. Keep your mind free of those negative emotions. Keep your mind clean and clear. Then it will function like a well-oiled engine.

Thought

Thoughts act like a steering wheel, taking you wherever you want to go in life. Thoughts help you change your state of mind. *You can steer yourself either to positive feelings (i.e., a peaceful and joyful state of mind) or negative feelings (i.e., an unhappy and distressed state of mind) depending on where you focus your thoughts. Focusing on good thoughts lead to good feelings, and a focus on bad thoughts lead to bad feelings and we can consciously make that choice.*

Let's say you are a Democrat. When it comes to elections, **thinking** of all the reasons why Trump is wrong and how terrible he is for our nation and watching all the TV channels that bash him, **is going to make you feel stressed. The more you think about it, the more negative feelings you are going to create within yourself.**

Bashing Trump may initially give you pleasure but soon all that negativity will catch up with you like a firestorm and burn you out. So, I advice that you **minimize your exposure to negative information. Don't focus on negative thoughts. Don't think them.** Rather, steer yourself away from them, whether it is by turning off the TV, doing something productive, or by choosing to watch something else that gives you good feelings.

Sometimes, you may accidentally get caught up in bad thoughts and feelings after arguing with friends/family over elections, reading a raging Twitterstorm, or watching a Presidential debate. But that doesn't mean that you have to stay in that negative state forever. *What do you if you are caught in a bad neighborhood? You turn your wheel and go away from there. Isn't it?* The same way, excuse yourself away from any bad situation. Stop reading things that do not help you. Turn your attention away to something else that is good for you. That is how you get back to a positive state of mind.

Remember, you are the power behind the steering wheel of your thoughts. You direct your thoughts to where you want to. At every turn of life, you have a choice: to turn toward good or to turn toward bad. The more you practice making this choice, the easier it will become to navigate yourself to a good state of mind.

It is by using the power of thought that we *create* good or bad in our lives, that we *feel* happy or sad, and that we *live* peacefully or miserably. So, take control of your life *now* by taking control of your thought power! **Realize that you are the creator of your thoughts and thus your emotions.**

Here is a practice that helps you stay peaceful during this election season: If you want to read and watch all the news you want, do it. But realize that they are simply someone else's thoughts, whether negative or positive. Whether they are talking or writing, they are using their own thought power to do so. It's their reality and they can think whatever they want. It doesn't have to be your reality unless you decide to keep focusing on them. **You see, you create your reality based on the thoughts you focus on.**

Let this truth sink deep within.

Consciousness

Consciousness is the awareness of your life and its experiences. Consciousness is like the windshield and windows of a car. It's **the window through which you experience life.** It informs where you are, what is happening within and around you, and whether you are at a desirable place in your life or not.

Agitated thoughts bring down your awareness levels. When your consciousness is low, it's like a car covered with frost. You can't see through the windows. You get into accidents. The same way, **clouded consciousness is dangerous because you make mistakes and get yourself into trouble.**

Let's say, you are a Republican and you saw Nancy Pelosi tearing off Trump's State of the Union Speech. Your blood boils with anger. You feel that's so disrespectful and disgraceful. In that mood, you walk out of your home and get into your car and as you drive away rashly, you totally fail to notice an oncoming car and you crash into it. That's how most accidents happen. When your mind is agitated by restless thoughts and negative emotions, it reduces your awareness levels, and the next thing you know is that you find yourself in trouble.

As the restless thoughts in your mind settle and you become calmer and calmer, your consciousness becomes clearer and clearer. You suddenly realize and regret what you have done. Many crimes happen this way. That's how we spend our life... moving from one restless state to another to another with only brief periods of calmness in between.-

So, arrest restlessness. Do not let things agitate you. Maintain an even state of mind, no matter what's going on. Practice this every day and you will be fine through this election season," concludes Dr. Calm.

The couple respond, "That sounds good. Thanks for sharing. We will try to implement these teachings. But sometimes things happen that drag us down to bad moods. What should we do then?"

"That's true. No matter how knowledgeable we are, there are times we just can't control our thoughts. Thoughts are like wild horses. They drag us down to bad emotions if not controlled.

But controlling thoughts is hard. I will share with you a couple of relaxation exercises that will help you calm down during tumultuous times."

The Two Relaxation Exercises: The Golden Art of Letting Go

Letting Go—The Only Way Out of Stress

Dr. Calm continues, "**A major problem we all face is the difficulty in letting go of negative thoughts. It feels like your mind has a propensity to cling tightly to negative thoughts.** Negative thoughts are tenacious. Sometimes, however hard you try, you find them stuck to you. Most of your stress would be gone if you could allow those thoughts to pass. **Breathing exercises have a powerful, calming effect on your mind.**

Imagine that you are driving to work, and on the way, you see an accident. You don't stop. You see that the police and the EMTs are taking care of it. What happens if all the drivers passing by notice the accident and pull over? There would then be severe congestion on the highway. The accident victims might be more difficult to reach. Likewise, if you obstruct the flow of thoughts on the highway of your mind, it leads to stress. All you have to do is, ignore negative thoughts and move on. **Negative thoughts are accidents in your mind. Leave them alone and they will disappear, and you will be fine.** By doing so, the traffic of thoughts in your mind will automatically return to normal flow, and everything will fall into place.

The Ancient Connection between Your Breathing and Thoughts

As Breathing Is for the Body, Thinking Is for the Mind. Your breathing and thinking are closely related to each other. Rapid and shallow breathing leads to rapid and shallow thinking, too. When you breathe rapidly, your body feels stressed. There is increased demand on your bodily organs. Lactic acid and other toxins accumulate and cause fatigue. In the same way, when your mind is racing fast with restless thoughts, you will feel mentally stressed, tired, and irritated. This leads to mental fatigue. **As you rest your body when fatigued, so you also need to regularly rest your mind to avoid overuse and fatigue.**

Knowing this connection between breathing and thinking, ancient saints of India discovered breathing exercises that calm the body and mind. **Because thoughts are subtle and hard to control, an indirect way of controlling thoughts is to regulate breathing.** When you breathe slowly and deeply, automatically your thinking slows down, too. It rests your body; your mind feels relaxed and calm.

The following are the two relaxation exercises of the P-E-T System. **When you feel that your thoughts are out of control and agitated, just sit down and practice one of these relaxation exercises. You will be pleasantly surprised by their strong, calming effect.** I recommend devoting 5 to 10 minutes to each exercise. However, in certain circumstances, when a longer length is not possible, even 1 or 2 minutes will produce a marked result if done with complete focus. Many times, during my life, I have used these relaxation exercises to great benefit.

Exercise 1: *Complete relaxation of mind and body with the breath*

1. Lie down or sit back in an easy chair; completely relax both your mind and body. Just let go of everything—every thought, idea, limitation, pain, every past event or future worry, every feeling, just about everything that could possibly arise in your mind—and just relax completely and ease into your body and mind.

2. Breathe deeply and release your breath slowly. Again, breathe deeply and release slowly. Do it a few times—possibly for the next few minutes. You feel your body and mind relaxing. Just ease into your breathing.

3. Let your breathing take a natural rhythm and follow it. Your breathing will slow down and will become very enjoyable and relaxing. Ease into it. Let it be. Let nothing bother you at this time. You are alone. You are free. You are enjoying yourself.

a. Remind yourself that you have no limitations other than those you impose on yourself. As you breathe, notice that you can take only one breath at a time. Observe that one breath. Be in that moment, be in that breath completely.

b. Then release the breath slowly, naturally. Be completely with it from the beginning to the end of the exhale. Observe it. Then let the next breath in. And continue the cycle. As you continue to do this, your breathing will slow down, your thoughts will slow down, and your awareness levels will rise.

c. Whenever you lose the flow of observing your breathing, remind yourself that you can only take one breath at a time, that you can only either breathe in or breathe out; you can't do both at once. Then why jump forward and think about the next breath and the next moment? Stay with the breath and stay in the moment.

4. As you relax and ease into this state, you will feel all the restlessness in your body and mind completely dissolve. If you still feel a bit of restlessness, continue to ease into your breathing. Just let it be. If you want to, observe your breathing as it naturally happens.

5. Doing this exercise for 5 to 10 minutes is usually sufficient to completely relax you, but if you feel like you need to do it longer, that's fine, too. But within the first 5 minutes, you may notice yourself falling into a sleep-like state in which you are deeply relaxed.

6. Rest there as long as you feel like before you return to your normal self. You will wake up feeling refreshed and rejuvenated. Now your mind is clear, and you can carry on with your life and your daily activities.

Exercise 2: *A flowing meditation on your thoughts*

1. Every day as you walk, sit, or engage in any other activity, take time to notice your breathing and your thoughts. You can do this any number of times during the day. Remind yourself that your true nature is peace of mind. Remind yourself that your joy is within and is independent of all external conditions.

2. Whatever situation that you are seeing now is just a momentary reality. That momentary reality will have to pass, and in the next moment, a new momentary reality will emerge. And so on it goes.

3. Any reality is real to you only as long as you focus on it. The moment you let go of the previous thought, the next thought will come forward, creating a new momentary reality. So, your reality essentially changes from moment to moment as you move along your thought train, choosing the thoughts you want to entertain.

4. As you choose positive and constructive thoughts, your reality will mold itself in that same way. If you choose to focus on negative and destructive thoughts, your reality will change to be the same. It is entirely up to you what thoughts you want to entertain.

5. To be able to choose your thoughts—and, thus, your reality—it is important to be as self-aware as you can to be able to consciously choose the direction you want to take in life. This exercise develops that self-awareness."

"Let's practice them now, says Dr. Calm."

As he takes the couple through these exercises, they both enter a deep state of relaxation, almost like trance. All the thoughts in their mind come to a halt. They don't know for how long they have been like that, but they wake up refreshed after a while, as if from a good night's sleep.

"What happened?" they ask.

"You kind of fell asleep" replies Dr. Calm.

"What?"

"Yes."

"For how long?"

"Not long. 15-20 minutes, I guess."

"Oh! That feels good. My whole body feels relaxed. My mind is refreshed. This is what we are looking for!"

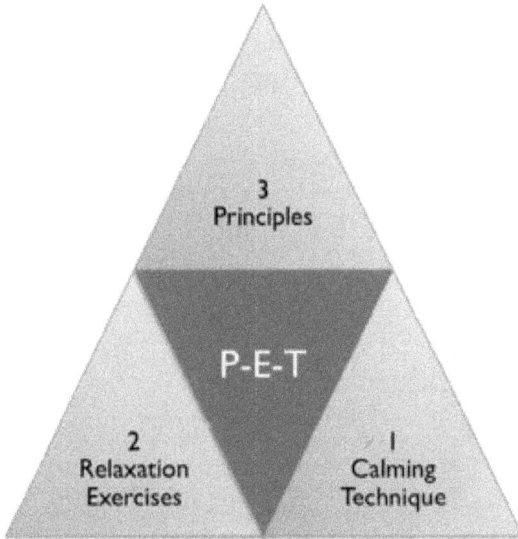

The P-E-T System

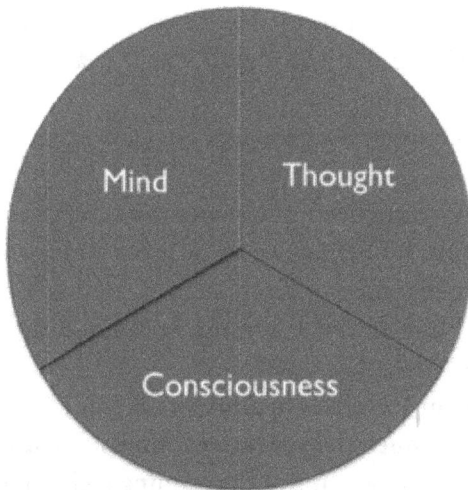

The Three Principles

Right Attitude	• Strong intention to feel deep peace.
Right Posture	• Sit erect, relax the body, close your eyes, and look into the third eye.
Right Technique	• ABC (Affirmation, Breathing, Concentration.)
Right Knowledge	• Agitated thoughts cause restlessness. Once they subside, you feel calm.
Regular Practice	• At least 20 minutes per day is pivotal for good outcomes.

The Essentials of Successful Meditation

Dr. Calm concludes, "Awesome! You could practice this exercise anytime you want during the day or night. Whenever you feel stressed and restless, do the exercise for a few minutes and you will feel better.

Alright, we discussed a lot today. I want you to go home and take some rest. In your next visit, I will share with you the last part of the 'P-E-T' system, the 'Calming Technique.'"

"So, how are you guys feeling today?" Dr. Calm asks the couple during their next visit.

"Doing great! We have been practicing the relaxation exercises every morning and at night. It's helping us to clear our heads and sleep better. I know today you are planning to teach us the Calming Technique. We are excited about it. How is the Calming Technique different from the relaxation exercises?" asks the couple.

"As the Relaxation Exercises begin to calm your mind, the Calming Technique takes you much deeper into calmness. These exercises prepare your mind for effective practicing of the calming technique."

The One Technique
The Golden Gateway to Deep Calmness

Calmness Is a Habit

Dr. Calm continues, "**Calmness is a habit and so is stress.** You may say that it is very difficult to remain calm. There is always something to disturb your peace of mind, isn't it? That's the reason we need to learn the right techniques that help us be calm.

People find it hard to attain calm because of the strong habit of restlessness that they acquire due to environmental conditioning since childhood. In this society, we rarely talk and teach calmness. That's not a part of our daily routine.

Without proper guidance, the human mind follows the path of least resistance and sulks in restlessness. Most people are not even aware that they are restless, and they live like that all their life thinking that it is normal. I did, too, until I discovered the power of calmness!

You may be thinking, "How am I going to arrest the restless monkey mind? Isn't it too hard to do that? Is it even possible?" Yes! It is possible. **With the right attitude, knowledge, and technique, it doesn't take much time to attain a state of deep calmness.** Daily practice of the technique described below will anchor you to the habit of calmness. And, **one day, your habit of calmness will become so strong that even the pandemonium of crashing worlds cannot unsettle you!**

The Right Technique at the Right Time

More than ten years ago, when I was experiencing extreme restlessness, one of my friends introduced me to a meditation technique. I had tried meditation before, but it did not work. So, I was initially skeptical. However, my need to calm down was so great that I was ready to try anything that could help me. *Necessity is the mother of motivation*! I quickly read the step-by-step instructions on how to practice meditation. I sat down in a quiet room and practiced the technique. I did not know what to expect but I nevertheless sat there for the next 10–15 minutes. Although my mind was restless, my effort was sincere. When I opened my eyes, I felt different. I knew something had changed in me. I felt calm. The negative thoughts that were bothering me for many days disappeared and were replaced by a subtle but clearly noticeable stream of positive feelings. My mind became impervious to the difficulties that enveloped me. All in all, I felt hopeful and good.

As I went on to carry out my daily activities, things started happening effortlessly in my life. People around me were nicer to me and more helpful than usual. As I came back home and started reflecting, I realized I had an excellent day, considering the grave situation I was in. As I continued to practice meditation more and more, I noticed that my life was on a roll. Along with feeling a deep sense of security from within, an intuitive inner voice guided me to the right opportunities at the right time, again and again. The end result was that in the three months following my first meditation, I was completely out of trouble and was carried to the perfect place that would unfold some of the most beautiful moments in my life.

In my mind, I developed a strong conviction that, **in the sea of life, hard work and perseverance—when compounded by the power of calmness—catapult you effortlessly to the shores of success and happiness.** Time and again, this truth was proved right in my life. Thereafter, I never looked back and never stopped meditating. I kept exploring more deeply the ocean of meditation. After much research, practice, and experience, I designed a unique technique that can be practiced by anyone regardless of their creed, race, religion, gender, nation, or any other identification.

The ABC Calming Technique

Use the ABC (affirmation, breathing, concentration) technique below for your benefit. You will reap the greatest benefit when you practice it regularly every day for at least 20 minutes, giving it your complete and undivided attention.

Some important points to remind yourself before attempting the technique:
• The good news is all problems have a solution.
• The key to finding solutions to problems in life is calmness.
• When you become deeply calm, automatically your inner wisdom comes forth and shows you the solution to your problems.

• When you need to find a solution to a problem, focus on becoming calm and then deepening that state of calmness to the point where all restless thoughts subside. Then you will be left with deep peace and joy emanating from within.

• In that state, you will find guidance and very clearly see what needs to be done. The Universe or God or greater power—whatever you want to call it—that force will come to your aid and rearrange your life situations to facilitate natural harmony in your life.

• If you learn to access that calm state of mind all the time, you not only solve problems easily, you will also prevent them.

• Practice this technique every day for the next 20 days, and great benefits will follow.

General Rules

1. Get up early in the morning (as early as you can, depending on your schedule).

2. Take a bath or shower.

3. Find a quiet place where no one can disturb you.

4. Practice the calming technique for at least 20 minutes.

5. The peak point of your practice is when you feel all the thoughts in your mind just disappear and you feel deep sense of peace (when you are there, you will know it—you will feel it).

6. Stay in that feeling of deep peace for as long as possible.

The ABC Technique has the following three components:

1. Affirmation: With deep attention, say to yourself, "I am calm" or "I am peace" or "I am joy."

2. Breathing: Take a few deep breaths (10–15 deep breaths), inhaling deeply and exhaling slowly. Be aware of the pause between inhalation and exhalation. If you can maintain the inhalation, the pause, and outgoing breath each to a count of 10 to 15, it will be most beneficial.

3. Concentration: Close your eyes and concentrate. Focus attention on the point between your two eyebrows. (See below for complete instructions.)

Affirmations with deep attention work because:

• Your attention is directed away from restless thoughts and that energy is instead used to focus on something positive and calming. The momentum built up by your restless thoughts dies away and is replaced by a calm feeling.

• We become whatever we focus upon. If we focus on negative thoughts, we tend to become negative. If we focus on positive thoughts, we certainly see more positivity around us. If we intend to become calm, we will become calm.

Please do not mistake intention plus deep attention with *controlling* thoughts. Here, you are not controlling your thoughts. You are merely focusing on one thought (of becoming calm) and letting other thoughts subside. Sometimes, letting go of worrisome thoughts happens easily and naturally. When it does not happen easily, then you need techniques to help you. Instead of fighting the thoughts, simply divert your awareness and energy to any other thought that is positive, *neutral,* and calming. That will bring peace.

However, do not focus on anything exciting. That will make you more restless. For example, if you imagine your ideal partner or a beautiful vacation destination, it initially might create a positive feeling, but if you continue to focus on it, it may lead to an obsession and a need to possess it; this, in turn, can lead to restlessness, as you keep thinking in your mind how to achieve what you want and whether you can achieve it, and so on. *The whole purpose of the calming exercise will then be in vain.*

The easiest and surest way to practice the technique is to choose a simple, neutral, and positive affirmation like calmness, peace, and joy. Love can also be used, although I prefer to avoid the word "love" because it means very different things to different people, which can lead to confusion.

With this effort, your mind immediately recognizes your intention to be calm and will stimulate the parts of your brain that assist you with this goal.

Specific Instructions

1. Sit straight either on a chair or on the floor. Make sure that your spine is erect, and your chin is parallel to the ground. Keep your hands, legs, and body relaxed. If possible, do not lean against the back of the chair or the

wall. If you have to lean against something to support your back, that is okay in these preliminary stages. But, where possible, avoid it.

2. Close your eyes. Take your index finger and touch the point between your eyebrows. That's your "spiritual eye," or "third eye." That's the point of super consciousness. *Mentally* focus on that point. Don't try too hard to focus; stay relaxed. (After a while, you will learn how to locate your spiritual eye mentally and there will be no need to use your index finger to touch and locate it physically. This comes with practice.)

3. Now, do the affirmation (the *A* component) as described above for 2 to 3 minutes. This will remind you of your true nature and the true purpose of doing this technique. Then do the breathing (the *B* component) as described above for 2 to 3 minutes. Doing the *A* and *B* components will prepare you to practice deep concentration and attain deep calmness. Then start concentrating deeply (the *C* component).

4. Initially, your eyes tend to drift away from the spiritual eye. It is because your eyes are habituated to restlessness as your mind is habituated to restless thoughts. There is a direct connection between the restlessness of your thoughts and the restlessness of your eyes. Once your eyes calm down and focus on the spiritual eye, automatically your thoughts will slow down, too. Likewise, once you learn to calm your thoughts, your eyes will lose their restlessness and will be able to calmly focus on anywhere you want with deep concentration. It takes practice to achieve such one-pointed concentration. With time, you will achieve it. Sometimes, this may happen right away and sometimes it may take a little effort.

5. Every time your mental focus drifts away from the spiritual eye, gently bring it back to that point. As you try and keep your mental focus on the spiritual eye, thoughts may restlessly dance in your mind and try to distract you. Don't let them. Regardless of what kind of thoughts they are, know that it does not matter; do not focus on them. Let them pass, as unattended thoughts will surely pass. Know that you are not your thoughts. Know that all thoughts are transient, and each thought creates only an illusory reality that is going to disappear when the thought passes. So, just let any thought that comes to your mind pass. Keep your focus on the spiritual eye.

6. To help keep your focus on the spiritual eye, I recommend chanting a neutral word or mantra. When your mind focuses on the mantra, it will more easily let go of the restless thoughts that are trying to distract you. With strong resolve and persistent concentration, keep focusing on the

spiritual eye, and at some point in time, you will suddenly find that all of the thoughts in your mind have disappeared as if they have been sucked out by a vacuum; that is, you will be in a calm state of mind. When that happens, and before a restless thought tries to disturb your mind again, stay there as long as you can. If you notice an uninvited thought coming back, ignore it, gently bring your attention back to the spiritual eye, and the restless thought will disappear. As you sink deeper into this calm state of mind, you will find great peace emanating from within and enveloping you from without.

7. Remain in this state as long as you can and would like to. Once you want to conclude your meditation session, before opening your eyes, ask for your problem to be solved. Sometimes, the answer comes to you immediately; at other times, the answer will come to you as a deep insight while you are carrying out your activities during the day. This may happen all of a sudden when you are not actually thinking about the problem. Often, you experience things suddenly falling into place, people becoming nicer to you, and obstacles in your path to success disappearing. You will have a much smoother journey in life than most people who don't meditate regularly.

The key to successful meditation is regularity. The more often and longer you meditate, the greater your happiness and success will be" concludes Dr. Calm.

Chapter 13
The Calm Activism

How to continue political activism and yet be calm.

The next few weeks are some of the most peaceful and fulfilled times in Johnny's parents' lives. It felt as if nothing, even the crashing worlds can disturb their peace. But, as time passed by, over the next few weeks, slowly they start feeling guilty within.

"We are sitting here in quiet and enjoying peace. But, what about the people out there? What about the constant fight between Republicans and Democrats? What about the policies that are harming our nation and endangering the environment because of global warming? How can we not be infuriated about it? How about the refugee crisis? What about the wars and recession? How can we help others? How can we stop the atrocities in the world?" the concerned couple reaches out to Dr. Calm for further guidance.

"So, you've been concerned. Hmmm...okay. Well, that's how life is. Even though we try to stay at peace, something comes up to challenge us. We are bothered by things around. **The only way to live is to gracefully handle our challenges while remaining calm within. It's the balance that is important.** If we try to do too much, soon we lose our calm. If we just want to sit idle and be at peace, our hearts would not let us do that. We feel like reaching out and helping people. Good...good...I am happy that you are thinking about helping others.

Past few weeks, you have learnt a lot. Let's take a step further and see the big picture. I mean, there is a lot to life than just the elections or what is happening around us. When we understand that, everything false into place, including our role when it comes to the elections."

"Sure. Dr. Calm. We are eager to learn more," both the wife and husband reply calmly.

"Great! Here are a few things to consider," Dr. Calm continues,

1. **"A greater plan exists for this Universe.** Have faith that all will be alright. We were being told for centuries, at every single point in the history that this is the worst it can ever be, and we will not survive. Yet after each war, each mayhem, each atrocity we as a humanity have survived. And we will do alright even after the election, no matter what the result is. Regardless of who wins, some things will be alright, and somethings won't be. Remember, we live in a world of duality. **Positives and negatives, good and bad, pain and pleasure, are an integral part of the making of this Universe. There is a Universal Plan.** Everything happens for a reason.

Dinosaurs were the mightiest of the animals that existed on this earth. Yet, they had to perish when the time was ripe. If not for the extinction of dinosaurs, evolution wouldn't have progressed the way it's supposed to be. Human beings would have never survived the dinosaurs if they coexisted. You see, everything happens for a reason. Enjoy every phase of your life. **The more you accept things as they are, the more you align yourself with the Universal plan, and the less you will be affected by the dualities of the world.** The way to do that is to practice even-mindedness. When you learn to say, 'it's okay', no matter what happens, automatically you will be relieved from the delusory effects of this dual world. You will remain happy no matter what.

You may ask, what is the Universal Plan? I say, 'whatever that's happening now'! No one can write down the plan and tell you this is exactly what is going to happen in the next thousand years. There are far too many variables that are out of our control and are not even known. Anything can happen. **What is known is a drop and what is unknown is an ocean. The problem with human beings is they are under a constant delusion that 'whatever they know intellectually is what all that is there'.** They make decisions, predictions, and plans based on 'what they know intellectually' only to find that at least half of the time, they are wrong. The Universe has its own plans.

The best example for 'The Faltering of the Predictions of Human Intellect' is the Nov 2016 election cycle. Based on all the polls, political surveys, and expert opinions, Donald Trump shouldn't have won. Starting from day one when he came down the escalators in the Trump Tower to announce his Presidency, they said again and again that he cannot win. They ridiculed him. They laughed at him. They mocked him. And yet Mr. Trump prevailed. What's all that about? Considering all the outrageous things Mr. Trump did and said on the campaign trail, including the 'Locker Room Talk' and 'I could shoot someone down in Manhattan and nothing will happen to me', he should have never won according to the intellectual analyses we made. Yet, he won. So, don't you think that there is a Universal Plan for him to win. I am absolutely sure there is one. The Universe wanted him to win, and he worked with all his strength and did his best to snatch victory away from the Democrats. **That quality in him, to work hard and do his best to win, despite all the negativity surrounding him, we must surely appreciate, whether you like him personally or not.**

I believe there is a reason Mr. Trump won in 2016. That's what the Universe wanted. Align yourself with the Universal plan and be at peace.

Now, fast-forward to 2020 election cycle, despite all the efforts by Trump, he couldn't win. The power, money, influence, and all the might he and the Republican party wielded at that time couldn't prevent the loss. Biden, despite the advancing age and concerns about his cognitive capabilities, won the Presidential election. But, let us see how the future unfolds for the next election cycle. I am sure, the Universe has its plan," smiles Dr. Calm.

The couple quietly listening until now, respond, "Hmm. It seems everything is happening for a reason. But, what about the global warming issue? This is one thing we can't digest. We still don't have enough policies to protect our environment and we are afraid of the future of our children, our nation, and the world."

Dr. Calm continues, "The concern you have is understandable. But I think everything will be alright.

2. The Earth is stronger than what you think. Yes, we should be mindful about how we use our resources on the earth and not abuse our environment. But do not think that the Earth survives because of human beings alone ... it's very egoistic to think that way. The earth has been there for billions of years prior to our existence and will remain in existence for billions of years more. I know that Global Warming can affect all of us. Many governments and big organizations are taking necessary steps to help reduce

Global Warming. But you are worried that the current policies are not enough to stop Global Warming. The question is, "What can we do about it? Is it within our control to do anything about it?"

In my opinion, if every person is simply more mindful, disciplined, and be a good citizen about using their resources wisely and not waste them, whether it is water, electricity, food, or something else, that by in itself will help us a lot. If they take responsibility for their own life, their happiness, and stop abusing the social system, that itself will create a revolutionary positive change. At individual level, everyone can do it if not for their bad habits that prevent them from doing it. These **bad habits lurk deep in our mind as long as we are restless and stressed.**

Stressed people, often do not realize their faults and if they do realize, they won't be ready to address them and will become defensive when someone tries to advise them. This is true whether you are a common man or a congressman. When they find calm, they will be able to change these habits.

For example, let's take something as simple as throwing the plastic bottles or cardboard in the recycling bin and throwing garbage in trash can. I have seen many households who do not do it. When I looked into the reasons, I found that the people in the household are too stressed and distracted. They are throwing whatever they want, wherever they want. It's a simple discipline that can help the environment if everyone does it right. The same with paper towels. We Americans waste lot of paper. The statistics show that to make one ton of paper towels, 17 trees must be cut down and 20,000 gallons of water are consumed. Multiply that by the 3,000 tons mentioned above, and you get roughly 51,000 trees and 60 million gallons of water—consumed every day. Just by being mindful we could save lots of paper and so trees. Yet, I see both at work and home, people using paper injudiciously. Again, it's the stressed out and restless people are the ones who have a difficulty in building a new habit to prevent paper waste. It's because they are consumed by life challenges and are too distracted to focus on anything else than their problems. Sometimes people get too defensive if we say anything about their paper wastage because their ego comes in the way. They are not ready to follow us even if it's a good advice. You see, if people are just mindful of their own habits and take responsibility for their behavior, it can bring significant change to our environment. **Ultimately, whether at organizational level or individual level, the greatest enemy to fight global warming is our own** ego, with its habit-bound waste producing behavior, not amenable to positive change because of defensive attitudes. This is true not just for fighting environmental issues but almost any issue that is detrimental to us as a society. So, I say the key to saving our environment is stress management. When people are calm, their egos dissolve, will be more open minded, less defensive, and more amenable to change. That is how collaboration flourishes and great ideas get a chance to be implemented. So, 'Calmness First!'" concludes Dr. Calm.

"Dr. Calm, whatever we say, finally you bring us to your 'Calmness First' slogan!" the husband says jovially, "How is that possible?"

"Well, I am not making it up," smiles Dr. Calm. "That's the truth. It's really 'Calmness First'. Only when we are calm that we reap true happiness and success in life. Calmness is the source of all positivity and creativity. The anti-thesis to it is stress. People who are habitually stressed, their lives fall apart easily. They reap misery and ultimately failure, both professionally and personally. If you simply observe the lives of people who are deeply calm vs. those who are constantly distressed, this truth will be evident. So, it's really 'Calmness First'" reiterates Dr. Calm again.

The husband now asks, "I have done some soul searching past few weeks. I am a lifelong Democrat. I find it hard to accept Trump. I am trying hard to be neutral towards Trump and be a moderate Democrat. But I am having a hard time in changing my perspective. Can you help me with that?"

"I am thrilled to hear that you are genuinely trying to be a 'Demo-Blican'. Sure, let's discuss," responds Dr. Calm.

3. Avoid the Blame Game and Maintain Objectivity. We should give credit to people where it is due and criticize them gently when it's truly warranted. Media has lost its objectivity. That's a huge problem not only in our country but many others. The media chooses to focus on all the negativities of one's Presidency, rather than reporting both good and bad with equal enthusiasm.

What I am saying is, **the media's lack of objectivity is making it difficult for us, the people, to know the Truth.** And maybe this is making Donald Trump more aggressive. May be if the media is more objective and gentler with Trump, there is a probability that Mr. Trump will scale back on his attacks. We all know that **Trump is not a typical American President, and he is not going to keep quiet and take the criticism without fighting back.**

When the media knows his personality, then why instigate him? How about cooling things down and making an agreement that neither of them (the media nor Trump) is going to be unreasonably critical of each other, will maintain objectivity, and will help each other to inform the American Public of the Truth, which is their highest duty?

Do you think that is going to happen? Most people would say that is never going to happen. Probably they are right. But as I mentioned earlier, I am an eternal optimist, sometimes to the point of being delusional :) I hope this happens. But we got to start somewhere. May be CNN, may be MSNBC, or may be FOX NEWS. Or may be a small media outlet starts being more objective and we all be supportive of them.

We the people also must learn to be more objective and not be carried away by our emotions. But that can only happen when we are calm. **When a man loses his calm, he loses his objectivity.** When a man is restless and stressed, he becomes defensive and doesn't want to listen to others' perspective, whether it is you, me, or Trump. When we are not calm, our ego is high and makes it difficult to get along with others. **If we can really get all our politicians, including The President, all the politicians, and other top officials, to consistently meditate and find calm, even for 15-20 minutes a day, it's going to entirely change the political turf in this country.**

Deep calmness brings forth some of the most beautiful qualities that we all are born with as human beings – forgiveness, kindness, understanding, selflessness, wisdom, good discernment, love, compassion, and many other qualities that can touch your opponents' hearts and make friends of your enemies. I strongly believe in this approach because I have seen that magic happen many times in my life as well as in my clients' lives.

We must always remember that no person is 100% bad or 100% good. We as human beings are an admixture of good and bad together. **The more we see the good in Mr. Trump, the more he will show the good side of him. It's true not just for Trump but for us all, human beings.** But it takes patience, forgiveness, kindness, truthfulness, and much more to be the beacon of change. Mahatma Gandhi is the greatest example for that. Martin Luther King, Nelson Mandela, and many other great ones have shown us the path to righteousness and freedom. We should follow in their footsteps as a nation, for our own benefit.

I believe that we will do well as a nation when 'Media' is held responsible for reporting the Truth as it is but not as they want to. No tweaking. No twisting. Don't we teach our children to 'not lie' and 'always tell the Truth?' Then why don't we hold the same standards to our politicians and media? Because we adults have become lenient towards ourselves and others, when it comes to being more honest and straightforward. We are insecure. We don't want to be exposed. **What we need as a nation is more of character building than concrete buildings.** It is the character of the people of the nation that is going to hold it strong during the times of political uncertainty and turmoil. The military is helpful when there is an attack from outside but not so when the attack is from the inside, because of foul politics, social unrest, and media favoritism. As long as greed and ego prevail, this problem cannot be solved. This can only be solved by nurturing an environment of selflessness. **When people learn to be deeply calm, their ego dissolves and selfishness flees. So, Calmness First! It's always Calmness First!!**" smiles Dr. Calm.

"So, it's again Calmness First, huh!" grins the couple. "But, how do we get people, especially the politicians to embrace it?"

"By helping them understand the True Purpose of their lives," answers Dr. Calm plainly. When people understand the true purpose of life, they will change."

"So, what's the true purpose of life?" asks the couple.

"Hmm. You are asking me this question after all the discussions we had so far. Come on..." jokes Dr. Calm and continues,

4. "The True Purpose of Life is to Find Lasting Peace, Joy, and Love. No matter who you are, where you were born, what race you belong to, what job you do, how rich you are, and which country you live in, this is the single most important purpose of our existence as human beings. No matter if you are a janitor or the President of the United States, it is important to keep this True Purpose always in mind and keep working on it. Have that at the core of your life plan no matter how busy you are and how many other activities that you are engaged in. It's because we all need to feel at peace, enjoy life, and be loved. People may say, oh we don't need all that...we just want money, we just want power, we just want a big home, or a nice car or something else but they want all that because they want to feel happy, peaceful, and secure. The problem though is that those possessions, power, and politics do not guarantee lasting peace, joy, and love. People may have all that but still be unhappy and miserable. See the people in Washington D.C. Do you think all these prominent and powerful politicians are truly happy? They are always worried, constantly fighting and fuming. I mean, they are so stressed. When you look at it that way, you suddenly lose the fascination of becoming a politician. Their lives are uncertain. It's a constant battle. You never know who is going to stab you from behind, politically. It's a constant threat in their lives.

Look at President Trump. It appears to me that he is upset with a lot of things. I could be wrong because I do not know him personally, but his happiness seems to depend on what happens on TV and who says what. But you can't always control what other people say about you. **If you are constantly bothered by what others are saying about you, you can't live peacefully.**

Even Jesus Christ was not liked by all. So, you, me, and Trump can't expect everyone to like, respect, and agree with us all the time. This world will say what it wants to, and you got to do what you got to. **If you could ignore criticism and keep carrying on with your work, not only will you be at peace with yourself, but you will garner respect.** It's a great quality that very few people possess. I really feel that Mr. Trump will quickly become Presidential and revered if he embraces this quality. It will enhance his image positively and **bigly!**

Now, coming back to peace, joy, and love, don't you think Mr. Trump and our politicians need them? Of course, they do. Don't you think they want to feel secure? Of course, they do. However, they think, like many others in this world, that it comes from outside. That it comes from accumulating more or accomplishing more. But that's the greatest delusion we all are led to believe by this world, because of our environmental conditioning that has been happening since were born. Trump has everything one can ask for...had a great life, has lots of money, name, fame, children who could carry his lineage, and he is even the President of the United States, the most powerful nation on the earth, at this time. If this doesn't quench his thirst for more, nothing else will. If this doesn't bring him to live peacefully and feel secure within, no other material achievement will. What then would give that to him? **How can Mr. Trump be happy, peaceful, and secure all the time? The answer is within him. By embracing the peace within. The innate health within. By realizing that which you**

are seeking is already with you. All you have to do is to turn your attention within to know it. Once you realize it, then all else becomes less important. In fact, I think that Mr. Trump is one man who is really qualified to embark on to this journey within, because he got everything else that a man can ask...money, popularity, power, and much more. He has nothing else to explore and prove. Actually, if he ever decides to embark on this inner journey, he will do even better if he is elected as the President of the United States," concludes Dr. Calm.

The husband immediately says, "Do you think he is ready for it? Don't you think he is too lost and too materialistic to pursue a spiritual path?"

Dr. Calm smilingly says, "Only Mr. Trump will know. Who are we to judge, to say that he is materialistic or spiritual? We do not truly know him. Only he knows who he is. And no one is unredeemable. Every person on this earth, including President Trump has equal chance to succeed in their spiritual quest, if they make a sincere and wholehearted effort. And here is the secret, **the farther you are from the spiritual path, the easier it is to see good results quickly!** That must be encouraging for those who are willing to embark on a spiritual journey."

"Wow! We like that idea of Mr. Trump being at peace with himself and others, embarking on a spiritual journey, and being able to ignore his critics. I mean that's going to be an earth-shattering change for all of us on this globe! Thanks for being so positive and hopeful Dr. Calm. Whether we achieve it or not is irrelevant. Just being able to consider the impossible and being optimistic about it itself is a great quality. Thank you again for all that you have been doing for us," merrily laugh the couple.

"It's my pleasure. I am here whenever you need me," replies Dr. Calm.

And with that, they adjourn.

Chapter 14
Bringing Together the Divided Nation

Johnny and his family get together to start a grassroots movement to bring together the divided nation.

The couple goes back home. That night, even though they personally feel at peace, they still find it difficult to sleep. There is a pressing question on their mind, "How do we contribute to bringing together the divided nation? What can we do as responsible citizens to bridge the gap between Democrats and Republicans?"

They both wake up with a strong determination to work on finding the solution to this problem. Every day they see people fighting over politics on TV, on social media, and in their community. They themselves were the victims of polarized political ideologies and were miserable because of the constant bickering due to their partisan differences.

The wife mentions that one of her colleagues was called a racist, sexist, and a foul-mouthed idiot by his neighbor for supporting Mr. Trump. This can't go on like this. **People can't be mean to each other just because they have a different political opinion.** Many Republicans, especially Trump lovers are totally furious about being mistreated and being called names just because they support Trump. I know of a woman who lost her daughter to an illegal Mexican criminal who shot her. I see why she supports Trump, who promised that he will fight illegal immigration.

The husband remembers his recent conversation with a cab driver, a Trump supporter. He tells his wife that, the moment the driver said he is supporting Trump for President this year, his Facebook friend count went down from 6000 to 600, overnight. His cousin called him and started cursing him.

The wife speaks of another incident, "One of the Republicans I know went totally ballistic when a Democrat friend of his was actively supporting gun control laws, after there was a gun shooting incident at her daughter's school. They have been lifelong friends until then, but their friendship went sour after this incident."

The husband resumes, "I have a young student who reports that he gets bullied at high school because his parents are Democrats. And you know Johnny's girlfriend recently broke up with him because Johnny decided to stay neutral to Trump instead of criticizing him like before. She took that to be disgraceful towards women."

"Our people seem to be extremely polarized on various issues. If we continue like this, our nation will be in huge trouble. Our communities will fall apart. Friends and family will be fighting against each other. This country, a free nation, has given us so much. We got to do something about it," the husband says patriotically.

"Yes, we need to do this for our people, our children, grandchildren, and the future generations" agrees the wife. "Let's ask Dr. Calm in the next visit if he would have any ideas to help us."

So, the couple calls Dr. Calm over the phone, "We have an important question that we forgot to ask during the last visit. We are politically active people. We always did things during the election time, and we want to do something this year also. But instead of doing something partisan, we want to do something that would help both sides of the aisle. We have been thinking how to do that. Any advice from you?"

Dr. Calm replies, "But only you could answer that question. What's it you would like to do for this country at this time? I am so happy that you want to help others and willing to think non-partisan. **It's important to take part in activities that are meaningful for your heart and soul. We all are born in a specific place in this world for a reason.** Just because we know how to be calm, it doesn't mean we just sit around and not care about what's going on in this world.

For example, my role at this time is 'helping people find calm during this election cycle so that they don't go crazy with all that media frenzy. If I could help them feel at peace, they could focus on their jobs and other important activities in their life. That's my goal for this election year, to help anyone who seeks me.' What's your role, you think?"

Both the husband and wife, at once exclaim, "**Demo-Blican! We feel like people need to be more moderate in their approach towards elections. Being extreme in either direction takes us only far apart from each other.** It is important to see the common ground. It's important to see the value of unity. People should use common sense to make decisions. **United We Flourish. Divided We Perish! That should be the slogan of the nation and its people,**" they complete their thought in an inspiring fashion.

Dr. Calm says, "Well, that sounds great but how are you going to bring the divided nation together? It's not going to be an easy task, but I like your Non-Partisan Political Activism."

The couple reply, "Of course, it's not easy but we will do what we can and will leave the results to the Universe and God the Almighty. All we can do is give our best. We may not be able to change what happens in Washington D. C., but we could change what happens in our neighborhood. We will think about it over the next few days."

"I like that idea. **Start small. Start impacting things within your reach first. See what happens and then go with the flow.** I think Johnny and his grandpa would enjoy this discussion too. Would you like to involve them? Let's all get together sometime next week, and we will sort this out" says Dr. Calm.

"That sounds amazing!" the couple reply excitingly. So, they invite Johnny and grandpa to their home that weekend. All of them sit together to discuss how to bring together their community and help them have a peaceful election season. After some preliminary discussion, they go back to Dr. Calm to further explore this topic. They all get together at a local restaurant.

Grandpa takes the lead, "Dr. Calm, nice to see you. I am glad that my son and daughter-in-law were able to find your help and benefited from it. They both are happy in their lives now. And here is my grandson, Johnny. You met him at the birthday party. It's Johnny's idea to originally begin this political discussion and help people who are stressing about the elections."

Dr. Calm smilingly replies, "Johnny, thanks so much for creating an opportunity for us to discuss this important topic."

Johnny quickly replies, "Thanks Dr. Calm but all the credit goes to grandpa. He told me his story during the 2016 election season and how you were able to calm him down. Then he went on to help my friend Billy as well as myself. And he is the one who suggested that my parents see you and made appropriate arrangements for that. Now, we all are happy as a family. And as mom and dad rightly pointed, we would like to help our friends, neighbors, and many other people in our community to reap the same benefit as we received from your teachings. We hope to bring together the divided nation, one community at a time and hopefully it becomes a big movement at some point of time."

"Johnny, I like yours and your family's noble and forward thinking to help others. Let's do it together. First, I think we need a strategy on how we want to reach out to people. Then, we need what we are going to teach them. Then, we must figure out how to make this noble effort go viral. We need to get support from the big organizations who share similar interest like ours, to help people find peace and fight stress during this election season. Then we take the next steps based on the opportunities that open up. An important thing to remember is that we need to make sure that we don't get caught up in the political turmoil and stress ourselves during this process. If we take that precaution, we should be fine," says Dr. Calm.

Johnny's parents say, "We agree. So, what should be our strategy? I think we need to compile all the important teachings we learnt together into small booklets, make some flyers displaying our message, post it on social media as well as in the neighboring communities and organizations, and look for people with similar ideology to help us spread the message. We should remain strictly non-partisan and help people on both sides to find calm, Republicans and Democrats. If we help them find calm, that itself will take care of the rest. As Dr. Calm says, **when people are calm within, their inner wisdom will show them the right thing to do. They will be guided automatically to be nice, kind, and non-judgmental towards others.** Such positive behavior will resolve the divide between people and make them united. What do you guys think?"

"That sounds great!" all three, Johnny, grandpa, and Dr. Calm exclaim.

Grandpa replies, "I have a suggestion to add on to this strategy. How about each of us make a determination to personally help at least one person during this election season and ask that person to do the same for another one? For example, I helped Johnny. Johnny helped his friend Billy and his parents were helped by Dr. Calm. Now the parents want to help others. You see, when we help people wholeheartedly and they are truly impacted, they will be willing to help others. I think that's the fastest way to impact people's lives, by word of mouth."

"I think that's a brilliant idea Grandpa. But what are we going to teach them? How are we going to direct them to the resources they need? Not everyone can spend hours and hours to come see Dr. Calm nor everyone has a wise grandpa to help them. How about we create some audio and video that people can access whenever they want. It could be in the form of a podcast too. We can have these videos available on YouTube and other social media platforms," Johnny proposes.

"That sounds great Johnny," all three agree to that.

"Dr. Calm, can you put together a short booklet with your teachings that's easy to digest for people during this election season?"

"Sure," replies Dr. Calm. "I will work on it this weekend and will get back to you. Meanwhile, let's discuss about divisiveness a little bit and understand where it is coming from. That will help people overcome it."

Dr. Calm continues, "There are two components to divisiveness, individual and Universal. Let's start with the Universal aspect of divisiveness. This Universe came into existence because of divisiveness. Divisiveness means nothing but differentiation. In the beginning there was just One. The One has become many because of divisiveness. **The One had to divide Itself into many so that we all could be manifested. That's how the creation started.** If the One is not divided, we wouldn't exist. Neither you, nor me, nor animals, plants, planets, stars…essentially nothing would exist. So, we must respect the divisive aspect of the Universe. Without the divisiveness, there would be no Universe for all of us to enjoy. There would be no drama. There wouldn't be any romance between man and woman. There wouldn't be any interplay between man and the nature. There wouldn't be any science or technology. There would be no movies or TV shows. Life would be boring, isn't it? So, some divisiveness and variety are essential for life to be enjoyable, at a physical level. So, **divisiveness is not bad when you look at it as just diversity that is essential for life.**

However, **it is bad when human beings, driven by ego, purposefully create divisiveness.** That's individual divisiveness. Such divisiveness is instigated by volatile comments and hypocritical behaviors. **Divisiveness is what keeps politicians in office despite their shortcomings. Divisiveness is what keeps us, the people conflicted.** Solving this divisiveness is essential to help people come together and be united.

Solving divisiveness starts at an individual level. See if you can be neutral to people around you, no matter what they say about Trump, Biden, or some else running for elections. Respect others' perspectives. Treat them as fellow human beings, regardless of who they support politically.

We are unnecessarily fighting with each other, bringing misery to our lives. We all should realize that if we remain divided, politicians will benefit from it. They thrive on our divisiveness. That's the reason they divide and rule. If we all stay united, they got to do everything we ask for, isn't it? Divisiveness is not going to help us get along well with our family, friends, and colleagues. It creates conflict in our communities and organizations, making us even more divided as a nation.

If divisiveness and fighting with each other helps, let's take out our swords and slash each other. Let's take out our guns and shoot each other. What do you think is going to be the outcome? Terrible, isn't it? Looking at the middle east and politically unstable regions of the world, it's clear how bad the situation would be. Isn't it? Did it help them? No right?

We have such a beautiful country with vast natural resources, nice people, advanced technology, great scientists, and much more. We have great freedom in this nation. **We must use our resources and freedom to help each other to grow and live happily. We need to work collectively as a nation leaving behind our differences.** But this is not what we are seeing. The nation is constantly at war, because of divisive politics. **So much of our energy is being wasted in this constant war of minds between the political elites, fueled by media sensationalism, and supported by ultra-rich corporations.**

Can you imagine how much energy can be saved if Democrats and Republicans are in harmony with each other? Can you imagine how much synergy will there be and how fast we all can progress as a nation?

The Root Cause of Divisiveness

So, what is it that causes all this divisiveness? It's the **EGO. Until ego rules, there will be divisiveness. Ego likes the idea of separation. Ego thrives on separation.** It creates the concept of you and me and that you are not better than me and I know better, I can do it better, I am taller, I am stronger, I am superior, you are inferior, and so on. We learn this from a very young age, as children. We get our egos constantly boosted by our parents, friends, family, teachers, and even strangers.

As we grow up and when we are not these little adorable children, the world is not anymore so flattering to us. We find that people are not anymore praising you for every little thing you do, like they did when you were a child. You have to earn the praise. You have to win their hearts. Otherwise, you are not anymore worthy. That's the concept we grow up with. If your teachers, parents, and others do not praise you, you think there is something wrong with you. You are constantly seeking attention. This is especially true in America. **Those who praise you and agree with you, you think are your friends and those who do not praise you and disagree with you, you think are not your friends. That's the beginning of divisiveness in us as little children.**

Divisiveness, at a social level is mostly based on agreements vs. disagreements and liking vs. disliking. But the truth is, **not all those who disagree with us or disapprove of us are our enemies.** Not everyone has to agree with us. It's just not possible for everyone to agree with us because we live in a world of separate realities. Each person is creating their reality based on their own thoughts and they are free to think whatever they want. So, **it's foolish to expect everyone to agree with us. It's equally foolish to think everyone should like us.**

Some people never come out of the child phase of their lives mentally, even though their bodies have grown. For some reason, they are stuck at a toddler or teenager level from an emotional standpoint, constantly seeking for approval and adulation. If they are not, they get into fight with others, perceiving that they don't like them. They feel conflict and tension with those people. This mentality and behavior continue until they **realize that true security, true approval, and true love, originates from within.**

It's finding the inner security that is most important if you need to resolve conflicts with others. When you realize that what others think and say about you matter less, compared to what you think of yourself and how you perceive yourself, all the conflict falls away. The divisiveness goes away.

When you are feeling secure from within, you do not feel threatened by every other comment that you see on TV or social media. You continue your work, unperturbed. For those people who are deeply stuck in the conflicted and divisive mode, for this to happen, deep soul searching has to happen. They need to feel peaceful and content. They need to access the deep calm with in. Then we have hope. Then the dissolution of ego starts and divisiveness fades. Harmony reigns.

The divisiveness in politics has its roots in the egoic separation in the minds of the people. Divisiveness is seen and propagated at three primary levels in any nation.

1. Political divisiveness
2. Media divisiveness
3. Social divisiveness

But the nation is comprised of people. Even politicians are people. So, it is the people that need to change at an individual level for the national and political divide to dissolve. **All divisiveness ultimately arises from individual egos and the feeling of separateness. Until we lessen our egos and let go of the illusion of separateness, we can't solve this divisiveness.**

We need strong leaders, not just politically, but also spiritually, mentally, and ethically, who could bring the nation together and heal the divisiveness. And it's not about just one leader but many leaders of that caliber in politics, business, media, and every other section of the democratic society. **As long as the society and the individuals of the society are being driven by ego, you cannot attain harmony. Period!**

The work for this kind of massive undertaking should start from the ground level, laying a strong foundation for it by building strong character in our younger generations. For that our family structures have to be strong. For that our greed levels must come down and we should spend more time with our families and friends and children. We should focus less on us and more on the welfare of our children.

It's an illusion we all believe in that our kids will be fine and will do great if we just provide them with lots of money and all the resources. Though that helps, it's not sufficient. **There is no replacement for strong character building and patient and careful nurturing of young minds. This should start at home and should be reinforced in our school system.** We need to help these innocent little ones transform into strong, wise, and loving adults like we carve out beautiful jewels from raw diamonds. For that we need to focus less on us and more on our children. For that we need to lessen our egos and be more self-less and giving.

Our innocent little children come into this world because of us, and they endearingly trust us to show them the way to gracefully handle this world. We must take that responsibility seriously. We need to parent them properly. But if parents themselves are stressed and unhappy, how can they help their children? If our school systems are stressed, how can they help our little ones? If political parties are stressed and constantly at war with each other, how can they help us, the people? You see, everything is inter-linked.

The only real solution to all these problems is to bring down the stress levels and help people be calm. And the reform must happen at multiple levels for us to move from being divided to united. When calmness prevails, stress retreats, and ego dissolves. So, Calmness First!

For this to happen, we need help from our politicians, our media friends, our family, society, organizations, and more. We need to realize that we all are in this together. Our individual development affects societal and national development. And our national and societal development helps us develop individually. It's interrelated.

The first thing that people need to realize is, the most important goal for all of us as a society, as a nation, and as humans is to raise above suffering and to find lasting peace, joy, and contentment in life. Such lasting peace and joy cannot be found on a material plane. Can only be found on a spiritual plane. For that we need to realize that we are not physical bodies. We are spiritual beings who have come to this earth for a human experience, and we have to go back to our home, the heaven, the abode of eternal peace and happiness. But we won't go back there if our actions are detrimental to the self and others. Only when we find harmony within and with others, we will progress to the next level in life. Until then we have to work on our own selves, our attitudes, our quirks in the personality, and iron them out before we reach our eternal home. One lifetime may not be sufficient for us to perfect ourselves and you may have to come back on to this earth again and again until you learn the lessons needed and perfect yourself to graduate and enter the heaven and stay there permanently. But we can start that process now, by learning to be more selfless, giving, and compassionate, extending our hand to help all mankind, and considering all people to be our own, one large family. When we do that as individuals, as a society, and as a nation, world harmony is surely attainable.

But what is it that is preventing us from doing so? It is the lack of understanding of our true selves, of who we are at our core, the infinitely potential self that is an undistorted image of The One Spirit, The God. Because of that ignorance, man tends to think that he is incomplete, he needs something else to fill that void...the feeling that he needs to add things to him and his life, whether it's money, name, fame, power, sex, wine, or something else so that he could feel totally fulfilled. But that total fulfillment cannot be found in any material achievements or worldly pursuits. That total fulfillment is only possible when he sees a glimpse of who he actually is and comes to the realization that he is complete. That he is whole and naught else need to be added to him. That realization can only happen when his mind is absolutely still. That happens when we learn how to subdue the restless thoughts in our mind and access the deep calm within. So, again, it's Calmness First!

When man realizes his True Self, all his compulsive desires fall off. But the desires that are in harmony with himself and the world around him, remain. Greed flees. Selfishness will be replaced by selflessness. Harmony and balance reigns. This we must teach people at all levels. For this, we must take help. We must start a grassroots movement. We need all the support we can gather from as many people and organizations possible. We need support at many levels, including:

1. Political
2. Media
3. Societal
4. Family
5. Individual
6. Organizational
7. International

That's how we are going to unite the divided nation. It's not going to happen overnight, but we can at least begin the process by sowing the seeds of calmness and harmony into the soils of people's minds," finishes Dr. Calm.

The whole family, Johnny, his parents, and his grandpa have been listening to Dr. Calm's discourse on divisiveness and how to bring together the divided nation. They have no further words to say. All they have to do now is, take action. If each one of them determines to help at least one another person and ask them to spread the message, that will be a good beginning. If they can have some of these materials available as books, audio, and video, that will help a lot to spread the message. Then they have to reach out to the media outlets and big organizations to help them spread this message of calm that is essential for people to survive the 2024 election without losing their minds. Dr. Calm said, he will create a small booklet with his teachings, over the weekend. Let's wait for it!

Chapter 15
Seven Effective Ways
To Beat Election Stress

A quick overview of how to remain calm during the election season.

Dr. Calm, as promised, puts together a booklet that encompasses his advice on how to evade the stress of the elections and stay calm during times of turmoil. Johnny and his family take this material to disseminate the teachings through social media, in their neighborhood communities, and more. Practice these 7 prescriptions from Dr. Calm every day for your benefit:

1. Prioritize Peace of Mind

a. Always keep in mind the true purpose of life, which is to overcome suffering and find lasting peace, joy, and contentment.

b. No one wants to suffer. Everyone wants to feel peaceful, secure, and happy. Learn how to make that possible in your life. If possible, help others do the same.

c. People falsely think that lots of money or material possessions or endless worldly pleasures are going to give them lasting happiness, but they ultimately fail you.

d. Realize that finding true happiness in material pursuits is like a mirage. It's illusory. Often, you drive yourself crazy in that process and lose your happiness and peace of mind. If you observe the rich people and celebrities of this world, this truth will be evident quickly. Many of them are stressed and unhappy despite their massive material success, name, fame, and Twitter following.

e. There is only one true way of finding lasting peace and joy in life. That is by prioritizing it, acquiring the right knowledge, and practicing what it takes to find it.

f. Realize that peace and joy are not things to be found somewhere outside you. They are within you. Peace of mind is your true nature. That is how you were born.

g. Innate Health is your natural state of mental well-being where your happiness is not conditioned to external circumstances. We are all born with this innate health, the ability to be happy unconditionally. That's your true nature.

h. If you observe little children, it will be evident that they are happy for no reason. However, as we grow into adults, we lost it because of environmental conditioning telling us that we can only be happy with certain conditions, whether it is having lots of money, nice car, big house, or something else.

i. Because of this conditional happiness, sooner or later we are prone to suffering when we lose what we have whether it's a broken relationship, loss of finances, loss of loved ones, or something else. The dependence on external circumstances for our happiness is the root cause of our suffering.

j. During the times of deep distress, when everything is lost in life, if you remember that what you lost is just conditional happiness and that your unconditional happiness, your innate health is intact deep within, you could bounce back from any stressful situation and find your happiness again quickly.

k. When it pertains to the elections, if you identify your happiness with the victory of your candidate, you are bound to be unhappy when your candidate doesn't win. It's alright to support and vote for anyone you think is appropriate but do not identify your happiness with their loss or victory. That's conditional happiness. Remind yourself that your happiness lies within. When you do that, you can be happy no matter who your president is.

l. Remember, your destiny depends more on what you do every single day in your life than who your President is. What happens in your house every day is more important than what happens in the White House when it comes to your daily successes and failures.

m. Stay strong, stay grounded, know who you are, relinquish conditional happiness, anchor yourself in peace and unconditional happiness, and you will remain unruffled during this election season. When it comes to elections, many things are beyond our control, but our happiness is still in our control.

n. Keep the true purpose of your life always in your mind, which is to overcome suffering and find lasting peace, joy, and contentment. Wherever you go and whatever you do, take this thought with you.

o. If everyone takes responsibility for their own happiness, most of the problems we face in this world disappear. But the selfishness and laziness that plague the human minds is the greatest hindrance for individual progress than which political party is going to prevail over the next four years.

2. Practice Presence

a. Most of us are distracted, hopping from one task to another, jumping from one thought to another, restlessly. Such restlessness is the key reason for unhappiness in life. Restlessness is the thief of happiness.

b. Our minds love to wander away from the present and either get stuck in the traumatic past or worry about the future. But remember that the past is nothing but a memory. The future is a figment of your imagination. It is not yet here. So, both the past and the future do not exist anywhere else except your mind.

c. Present is the only place where everything happens. Be present. Be in the moment. Be alert and awake. Then you will not be hurt by the illusory past memories, nor will you be worried about the imaginary future.

d. The more you dig into your traumatic past, the more you suffer from the resurfaced bad thoughts. Bury your traumatic past forever. We all have done mistakes in the past. You are not your past. Let it go. Learn from the past and move on.

e. When it comes to the elections, remember that imagining a fearful future doesn't help. None of us know who is going to win in November on the election day. The polls and the experts are not always right in predicting the wining candidate. So, don't be fooled by them. Simply choose your candidate and vote for him/her and wait for the results. Take one day at a time.

f. If you are a Democrat, you will be worried what happens if Trump wins. Will the world come to an end? Will there be rampant display of White Supremacy? Will he try to replace democracy with dictatorship? Will there be accelerated global warming? Will our cities drown and our kids and grandkids will have no future? The questions and scenarios that your mind can create are endless.

g. If you are a Republican, you are worried what if Trump doesn't win? Will there be a massive stock market crash? Will the economy enter terrible recession, like in 2008? Will the Democrats reverse the tax cuts? All the progress we made in the past, will it be lost? Are they going to make this country a socialist nation? There is no end to the havoc your mind can create by wandering into the future and frighten you.

h. You see, whether you are a Democrat or Republican, you have your own fear about the future. Our minds tend to project a fearful future and imagine the most terrible outcomes, but our future is not as dire as we often think! The worst possible situations we think usually do not come to pass by. Our mind needs restraint and proper guidance. That you must work on.

i. When your mind wanders into the future, gently bring yourself back to the present. Tell yourself that this is the only moment that is real. Everything else is just in your mind. Anchor yourself to the present.

j. Focusing on your breath is a powerful way to anchor yourself to the present. Do this small exercise. As you breathe, observe the ingoing breath. Then, as you breathe out, observe that too. Then again observe the ingoing and then the outgoing breath. Realize that when you are breathing in, that's the only breath possible. When you are breathing out, that's the only breath possible. You can't both breathe in and breathe out at the same time. That means there is only one breath possible at a time. That's the only breath, the only moment that exists, and that's real for you at that time. Focus on that breath, in that moment. That's the only moment present. As you do that, you will be deeply absorbed in the moment, strongly anchored to the present.

3. Learn to be Even-minded

a. Whether you are a Democrat or a Republican, remember that only one of the candidates can ultimately win the Presidential election. We don't know who is going to win. Do not create a fearful future in your mind about who is going to win or lose. Observe how it's going to unfold.

b. The truth is, if the Republican candidate wins, then Democrats do not win. If the Democrat candidate wins, then Republicans do not win. One of them must lose. Then, doesn't it make sense that you hope for the best and prepare for the worst? Doesn't it make sense that you get yourself ready to be happy no matter who wins? Then you won't be either too depressed or too elated when the results come out.

c. Let's learn to be even-minded. Even-mindedness means being poised no matter what, whether you receive good news or bad news. Remember that ups and down, good and bad, pain and pleasure are an inherent part of this world of duality.

d. Life is a roller-coaster ride. Ups and downs are natural. That's the nature of life. When you realize that, you won't get too excited when things are going well for you, as you know the next downturn is around the corner. And when things are not going well, you will not be too worried because the next upturn is around the corner. All you got to do is be patient and things will be alright.

e. When your expectations are not met, instead of getting upset, practice saying, "I don't mind." That is a good way to remain neutral to life's situations. When it comes to elections, prepare your mind to be poised no matter what the outcome is going to be. If you tell yourself that starting now, it becomes easier when the time comes to accept the election results, whether to your liking or not.

4. Maintain Strict Media Ration

a. Know that there is no end to media sensationalism. Anyone who observed the last election cycle and the events since Trump has won the 2016 presidential election, it will be evident that our media is ingenuous in creating sensational headlines on a consistent basis to pull people into watching or reading news.

b. The media networks are good at it because they have a whole team who work on how to make their shows addictive. They spend millions of dollars to make their programs entertaining and enticing. So, they are doing their job to thrive financially. It's a business and they do it well. It's their duty.

c. It's your duty, not to get pulled into sensationalism and consume all news with a pinch of salt. Ask yourself if what you read, listen, and watch is true or not. Try to obtain information form unbiased sources.

d. Know that most media channels these days are biased. To please their audience, they will have to cater to their needs and expectations. Or else their ratings will fall. For example, if a liberal media channel praises Trump on a consistent basis, most of their audience will turn off the channel. They watch some other channel that bashes Trump. The same is true for conservative media networks. If they bash Trump regularly, many Republicans will turn off the TV.

e. Unfortunately, it's just not the media but the people also have become so opinionated that they don't want to listen to things that they don't believe in. Many are not ready to explore the truth and consider alternative perspective. They rather live in their own bubble, in their own comfort zone. This is all because of the divisiveness stoked by the politicians, overly amplified by the media, and innocently perpetuated by us, the people.

f. Most of us do not know the truth about what really happens in the Washington DC. The truth is filtered by many, the journalists, the editors, the anchors, and their own biases and prejudices, before the news reaches us. As consumers and end users of TV/Radio/News magazines, all we have is a perspective. All we have is a distorted and diluted version of the original event.

g. Then why stress too much about media stories. Save yourself from stress and unnecessary headaches and heart attacks. Take all the information from media with a grain of salt. Be like a wise ant that only consumes sugar crystals, leaving behind the admixed sand. Use your wisdom to discern the truth from fake news. When your mind is calm, your inner wisdom blooms and you will be able to differentiate the facts from fallacies. Practice calmness.

h. Too much consumption of news is detrimental to your health. Your mind absorbs whatever information fed to it, innocently. Your brain becomes information overloaded and you will feel overwhelmed. So, avoid overconsumption of the information whether it is from TV, radio, magazines, internet, or social media. Save your energies.

i. Know that the same news is played again and again on the media channels, but in different ways and on different shows. You do not have to watch all the shows, spending hours and hours on TV. Pick your favorite show and stick to it.

j. Do not spend more than 30 min to a maximum of one hour a day on consuming news. That's enough time to get the gist of what's going on without getting dragged into the unnecessary details. But the media shows are addictive. If you can't restraint yourself from watching them, then you got to cut the cable.

k. The same goes true for social media. Do not spend more than 15-20 minutes a day on social media for consuming information. Do not participate in negative campaigns, commiserating with others. Stay positive on social media.

l. Do not think that the Facebook friend you are seeing is really happy just because they posted a happy picture. They may have their own troubles, despite putting on a happy face every time you see their posts. Do not compare yourself to others. Focus on your wellbeing, your career, health, and happiness.

m. Do not let the Twitter messages bother you. Do not let the Twitterstorms turn your life upside down. People could post whatever they want. It doesn't mean what they are saying is true.

n. Some people post on twitter, to just get attention or to divert the attention. You do not have to buy into other people's stories on Twitter. It's their reality, not yours. Your reality depends on what you think, not what others think of you.

o. The Trump you know from watching TV and social media posts may not be actually the real Trump. He may be different in person than what he is on TV. The media personality of Trump may be quite different from the private personality of Trump. If you never met Trump personally, do not take things for granted. And this is true for most of us common people.

5. Avoid Conflict with Friends and Family

a. No matter what happens in the politics, at the end of the day it is your family, friends, and colleagues that you will have to live with every day of your life. So, don't spoil your relationships with them over politics.

b. Neither Trump nor Biden are going to come to your rescue when it comes to your daily dealings in your life. It's your loved ones that will come to your rescue. Keep them near and dear to you.

c. When you discuss politics with friends and family, remember that each one of you have the right to your own perspective. Respect the other person's perspective.

d. Remember that we all live in separate realities, depending on our own personal thoughts about the issue. In any given situation, there is one absolute reality and many relative realities. When you realize this, you will feel less conflict with others. You will understand that everyone is creating their own innocent reality in their minds, often unknowingly.

e. A person's reality depends on many factors. The environment they grew up in as a child, the surroundings to which they are being exposed on a daily basis, their past experiences, present state of mind, and much more.

f. Always give benefit of doubt to people who I do not personally know, no matter what other people say about them. We truly do not know other people in our life, especially when we haven't had a direct interaction with them and haven't spent hours and hours trying to sincerely understand who they are. What all we have is our perception of them.

g. The reason why most relationships fail because either one or both of them never made the effort to truly understand the other...all they have is their perception of the other but not who truly they are. Where there is no understanding, there will be no love. Where there is no love, there will be only pretense but no true caring. Slowly conflict creeps in and ultimately the relationship falls apart.

h. We should not impose on others what we think is right, especially when we know that they hold a different position on that topic.

i. Most relationships fall apart because of false assumptions. These false assumptions often start trivial and slowly grow to giant differences in opinions, resulting in major conflicts.

j. Mantra for good relationships: avoid false assumptions, clarify when needed, and always try to understand. If you follow this, you will never fail your relationships.

6. Practice Calmness

a. If there is only one habit that you need to build in your life, so that everything else falls into place, that is the habit of calmness. When you are calm within, you automatically manufacture happiness from within.

b. When I say calmness, it is not just pretending to be calm but actually feeling the deep calm within, that we all are born with.

c. Unfortunately, that deep calm we all have within is masked by the restless thoughts. Restless thoughts are your greatest enemy to peace, joy, and contentment in life.

d. Most of us get habituated to restlessness because of environmental conditioning and because no one teaches us the importance of calmness in life. We learn a lot of things at school and college, but calmness is not one of them.

e. When our school systems, workplaces and organizations, and the society as a whole makes calmness a priority, we will find solutions to many of the social problems we face today.

f. A restless mind is foggy. When your mind is foggy, you run into all sorts of trouble. It's like driving a car in fog. You can't see clearly. You may get into an accident. The higher the density of fog, the lesser the clarity in moving ahead, and the greater the risk or getting into an accident.

g. We get exposed to a lot in our lives every day and our brains absorb everything around. It's our duty to unclutter our brain and empty our mind of restless thoughts. You do it by practicing deep calmness daily.

h. A calm state of mind is a good state of mind and, in that state, the thoughts that arise in your mind are positive and prosperous. Is that not what we all want in life? Be determined to remain calm no matter what. Even if people around you are restless, even when your surroundings are chaotic and when everyone is stressed out, you can remain calm, and you lead by example on how to remain calm.

i. At work or even at home, especially when you are stressed, take the time to practice the relaxation exercise. It helps de-stress. Take 5 minutes during lunch and do the exercise for your mid-day relaxation. Repeat the same at night for emptying your mind before sleep.

j. Never miss your daily meditations. If possible, do it the first thing in the morning, after taking a shower. If evenings are better for you, that's alright. Whatever time you decide on, do it every day the same time, if possible. That enhances the benefits you reap.

7. Empty Your Mind Before Going to Sleep

a. No matter how busy you are or how much work you have to do, ensure that you get 6 to 8 hours of sleep. Sleep charges your body and mind battery.

b. Can you imagine going to work during the day without charging your phone the night before? Your phone will stop performing and eventually will die on you. The same is true if you don't recharge your mind and body every night with sound and peaceful sleep; you won't be able to perform well during the day. You will be irritable, distracted, and error prone.

c. In the long term, people with poor sleep are at increased risk of experiencing heart attacks, high blood pressure, cancer, and ultimately death.

d. You may say, "How can I sleep well when the whole world is going crazy around me? How can I sleep well when every day there is some kind of bad news? As soon as I turn on the TV or read a newspaper, I am bombarded with negative information." I understand that it's not easy, but there are solutions.

e. *The first thing to do is to avoid being drawn into media sensationalism.* You only have 24 hours a day, and you already have so much to do. Why burden yourself with negative news? The world is not going to stop functioning if you stop watching news. Keep it to a minimum.

f. In particular, avoid watching or reading news for 2 to 3 hours before going to sleep. *All the information you absorb will overstimulate your brain, haunt you through the night, and prevent you from having a sound and peaceful sleep.* When you wake up in the morning, you can always catch up with the news if you want to.

g. A good way to empty our mind is by practicing the relaxation exercise and the meditation technique you learned earlier in this book. They help relax your mind, stop the restlessness, and instill calmness. *When your mind is calm and undisturbed, you will automatically have a sound sleep.*

h. *Later in the day, avoid beverages that could stimulate your brain, like caffeine, tea, and high-energy drinks.* Do not fall for addictions like smoking, alcohol, or drugs. They may give a feeling of temporary elation or sedation, but they mask the problem that is causing stress. In the long term, they are more damaging, than useful.

i. Do you know why most people can't sleep well even when they want to? It's because their minds are very restless with all the events and thoughts of the day. They just don't know how to shut down their mind. When they go to sleep, they carry those thoughts with them and thus have a disturbed sleep. During the day, they feel tired and sleepy and lack energy.

j. The real solution for good sleep is to arrest restlessness and find calmness. When you practice calmness using the Three Principles, the two relaxation exercises, and the calming techniques, you will automatically sleep well.

About the Author

Dr. Kiran Dintyala is an internal medicine physician, practicing full time in San Diego, California. He is an author, speaker and stress-management expert. He holds a Masters in Public Health (MPH), during which time he learnt his stress management skills. He is also a diplomate of American Board of Integrative and Holistic Medicine.

Every day he compassionately takes steps to alleviate the suffering of his patients/clients. He empowers them to succeed in their lives and to be happy, peaceful, and content.

His mission is to elevate the emotional well-being of the humanity, and thus increase the happiness index of the globe.

He strongly believes that with simple principles and techniques he teaches, anyone can become stress-free. He envisions and strives towards creating stress-free organizations, communities, and families across the United States and the rest of the world.

He believes a calm state of mind is essential for true success and happiness in life. He created the Stress Mastery Program and the P-E-T System for Stress-Free Living, to help people access 'Calm in the Midst of Chaos.' Some of the benefits of his teachings are:

1. Work-life balance
2. Peaceful & joyful living
3. Performance under pressure
4. Improved relationships at work & home
5. Relaxed & motivating work environment
6. Transforming organizational state of mind
7. Reduced absenteeism & presenteeism

A short version of my story

Many years ago, when I was in the spell of a perfect storm of stress in my life, I accidentally stumbled upon certain principles and techniques that saved my life. Those principles and techniques helped me calm down instantaneously and gave me the ability to take control of my life situation. That ability to calm down in the midst of chaos not only saved me from a dismal failure that threatened my career but also paved a path to the career

of my dreams. What I learnt over years through many life and death situations in my own life, I have put together as the P-E-T system for stress-free living. This easy to follow system melts away stress instantaneously. These principles and techniques work with mathematical accuracy!

Why am I doing this? Why did I choose this journey to create a stress-free revolution?

Having benefited from this system myself, now I am on a journey to help others. I know that stress is a relentless, silent killer. Having experienced extremes of stress in my own life, I know how it feels to be in a situation that makes you feel desperate, hopeless, and miserable. When you are in deep distress you feel that nothing works for you. You feel as if everything goes wrong in your life and there is no meaning to life. All the goals and dreams look futile. Yet, with experience I realized that no situation is hopeless and that there are obvious ways to emerge out of such situations successfully and find solutions to our problems. I am here to share with you what I learnt and be your guide to find peace, joy, and prosperity in life.

There is a need...a tremendous need to eliminate stress from our lives
Stress is recognized as a global epidemic by the United Nations. Stress management is corporate America's greatest challenge in the 21st century. Families are falling apart because of stress. Individuals are losing focus in their lives and rapidly moving towards failure and depression. Yet, there is not enough preparedness to fight stress in our current society. There are obvious ways to overcome stress and live a peaceful and joyful life.

Start your stress-free journey today!
The P-E-T system I teach is simple but powerful. You will be amazed by its tremendous positive impact, both professionally and personally! You will find how to be happy at home and work. You fill find innovative ways to transform your organization and your family in a positive way. You don't have to blindly agree with me. Experiment with this system. You will be pleasantly surprised!

For sales, editorial information, subsidiary rights information
or a catalog, please write or phone or e-mail

IBOOKS
Manhanset House
Shelter Island Hts., New York 11965, US
Tel: 212-427-7139
www.ibooksinc.com
bricktower@aol.com
www.IngramContent.com

For sales in the UK and Europe please contact our distributor,
Gazelle Book Services
White Cross Mills
Lancaster, LA1 4XS, UK
Tel: (01524) 68765 Fax: (01524) 63232
email: jacky@gazellebooks.co.uk

www.ingramcontent.com/pod-product-compliance
Lightning Source LLC
Chambersburg PA
CBHW070807280326
41934CB00012B/3097